TRUE NORTH TRADECRAFT

DISASTER PREPAREDNESS GUIDE

A PRIMER ON URBAN AND SUBURBAN
DISASTER PREPAREDNESS

-3RD EDITION-

BORIS MILINKOVICH, CD

DISCLAIMER:

"Although the author and publisher have made every effort to ensure that the information in this book was correct at press time, the author and publisher do not assume and hereby disclaim any liability to any party for any loss, damage, or disruption caused by errors or omissions, whether such errors or omissions result from negligence, accident, or any other cause.

This book is not intended as a substitute for the medical advice of physicians. The reader should regularly consult a physician in matters relating to his/her health and particularly with respect to any symptoms that may require diagnosis or medical attention.

The information in this book is meant to supplement, not replace, proper & professional survival and emergency preparedness training. Like any activity involving survival, equipment, austere and environmental factors, survival and disaster preparedness poses some inherent risk. The author and publisher advise readers to take full responsibility for their safety and know their limits. Before practicing the skills described in this book, be sure that your equipment is well maintained, and do not take risks beyond your level of experience, aptitude, training, and comfort level.

The author and publisher make no guarantees as to the efficacy of the methods described and make no guarantees that by following the methods described in this book that one will absolutely survive a disaster. These are opinions only and cannot cover any and all possible eventualities which one may face. Therefore, the information contained herein is for *informational & entertainment purposes only.*"

THE TRUE NORTH TRADECRAFT

DISASTER

PREPAREDNESS

GUIDE

A PRIMER ON URBAN AND SUBURBAN

DISASTER PREPAREDNESS

-3RD EDITION-

BY: BORIS MILINKOVICH, CD

All photographs are the property of Boris Milinkovich and used by permission.

Copyright © 2022

FIRST EDITION © 2018

ISBN: 9798356980350

PUBLISHED BY TRUE NORTH TRADECRAFT PRESS LTD.

TORONTO, ON, CANADA

No part of this publication may be reproduced, stored in a retrieval system, or transmitted, in any form, known or unknown, or by any means, electronic, mechanical, photocopying, recording, or otherwise, without written permission and consent of the author.

ALL RIGHTS RESERVED. © 2022

AUTHOR BIO

Boris Milinkovich, CD, has spent over 24 years in federal public service. He has served with the Canada Border Services Agency (CBSA) as a Customs Officer and with Transport Canada's Security & Emergency Preparedness Division as an Inspector operating in Marine & Aviation Security, Emergency Preparedness, Training & Liaison at Canada's largest and busiest airport.

Boris has also served as a member of the Canadian Armed Forces (Reserve) in a Light Infantry Battalion, the Intelligence Branch and with the Military Police since 1998.

Currently, he is the President and training director at True North Tradecraft Ltd., an independent security consulting firm providing specialized training in non-destructive covert methods of entry, counter-custody, personal security tradecraft and urban disaster preparedness for responsible and security-conscious citizens, as well as Military & Law Enforcement units.

He is also an associate urban survival & disaster preparedness instructor with WSC Survival School in Ontario, Canada.

Boris makes his home in Toronto, Canada.

DEDICATION

I would like to dedicate this to my family. My wonderful wife, Renee, for putting up with me, editing like a champ and being so supportive. My daughter, Petal, for always coming to "help" me while working on this project, and Liam, Indie and Nikki for their patience and support. As well, I'd like to thank my Brother, Rob, for his input, support and advice and my Mom for providing moral support. I'd like to also acknowledge the start my late Pops gave me in these matters. Always talking about how improvisation and preparedness are a key cornerstone of survival and life in general. Thank you Pops. And lastly, to my friends who were always there for me. Thank you all.

Acknowledgements

I would like to thank the following people for their professional critique, support and assistance:

Renee S., Arjeh V.S., Sam Garito (RIP)., Dr. M. Seidl, MD, TJ., Ace, Michael O., David Arama, Rob P., Karl O., Aaron C., Larry C., my friends from the Special Projects Community, The Treble Victor Group and the entire crew at Prince's Trust/Prince's Operation Entrepreneur (www.buyveteran.ca) for giving me the opportunity to build a foundation for success.

Introduction

Why was this book written? What is my purpose in doing so? Who am I to write anything?

Good questions, all. I am writing this primarily because I believe that people should take responsibility for themselves – that the government is not able to be in all places at all times to help everyone when disaster strikes. This is never as true as it is in a time of crisis. Everyone needs help but not everyone gets it. Resources get stretched thin. Circumstances such as weather make reaching those in need impossible sometimes. Therefore, I would like to give you a basic guideline to put in place to cope with a disaster should one occur. Though no kit is foolproof and no guarantees can be made, it stands to reason that any level of pre-positioned preparedness will increase your chances of making it through an ordeal unharmed. Many people I have spoken to state that the reason they do not have any preparations in place is because they don't know where to start They think it's too complicated, too expensive, or that if something does happen, the emergency services (or the army) will come and save them.

This publication's aim is to give the everyday person a starting point, to build a buffer of comfort and safety. It is only as complicated as you make it, and there is little reason why some thoughtful preparations for a time in need cannot be implemented by just about anyone. The basics should already be in your home, you need only organize yourself so as to have them readily available should something happen. Your planning can be effective, as expensive as you want to make it and you can ultimately put yourself in a position to help yourself instead of relying on others who may not come in time.

This book is about taking viable and effective preparedness principles and applying them holistically to your specific situation. There is no one-size-fits-all solution for preparing for a disaster. What is universal are the elements of planning, priorities and principles needed to effectively mitigate the risks posed by events of this kind. If you understand the risks, the principles and process for planning, then you can tailor your plan to meet your needs and build resilience in the face of adversity.

As for who am I to speak to these things, I'm certainly not the end-all-be-all. However, I do have over 20 years of service with various government departments (Military, Customs, Security & Emergency Preparedness) and years of personal time invested in being prepared, implementing preparedness plans for myself and government/industry, training others to do the same, learning continuously and constantly testing new information. As a family man, I would hate to see people get hurt or killed needlessly...especially if something as simple as preparation could save them. I do this for my kids, for my family, for you and for yours. I believe being prepared for an emergency or disaster is every parent and every citizen's responsibility. Take responsibility for your safety, make a plan, work the plan and make it through. Nothing in these pages constitute any sort of guarantee. Nothing is for sure, except death, taxes, and endless construction along the inner-city roads of Toronto.

"When seconds count, the police are only minutes away" (Unknown)

Be Prepared. Stay Crafty.
Boris Milinkovich, CD
Toronto, Ontario, CANADA
August 2019

Table of Contents

AUTHOR BIO iv

DEDICATION v

Acknowledgements vi

Introduction vii

PSYCHOLOGY OF SURVIVAL AND DISASTER PREPAREDNESS 1

DISASTER PLANNING 4

Survival Priorities and A Multi-Tiered Preparedness Strategy 22

SHELTER 30

FIRE, HEATING & COOKING 36

WATER 44

FOOD 52

MEDICAL & FIRST AID 57

HEALTH, SANITATION & HYGIENE 66

COMMUNICATIONS 72

LIGHT, ELECTRICITY & BACK-UPS 76

SECURITY 83

SPECIAL CONSIDERATIONS 97

ADDITIONAL CONSIDERATIONS & FOOD FOR FUTURE THOUGHT 108

Preparedness Recommendations 116

PSYCHOLOGY OF SURVIVAL AND DISASTER PREPAREDNESS

Without the Will To Live, your chances of survival are drastically reduced. It is the mindset, the drive, the desire to live and to make it through an ordeal, which often separates those who make it and those who do not.

There may come a time when there will be indicators of an imminent event occurring. Being aware of the world around you, be it local, regional, national or worldwide, is of paramount importance. Be aware of things like your local weather forecasts. Read or listen to the news – know about the world you live in. Shed your apathy and take responsibility for your safety and that of your family and loved ones. As was seen during the events leading up to Hurricane Katrina in 2005, the State response most people relied upon simply did not come. Those who had prepared for the coming storm weathered it far better than those who had not, so take responsibility for your own well-being. Prepare now so you can be confident later. Don't rely on others. Rely on yourself. Remember, things are replaceable, lives are not.

Maintaining a positive attitude and sense of humour are of paramount importance. Many times, these things alone have turned the tide of a survival situation from death to life. These traits are the temperance against panic. And panic is the ultimate catalyst of situations from bad to worse. Inevitably, panic invites the "**Seven Sisters of Death**" to spend time with you.

These "Seven Sisters" are:

- Fear
- Hypo/Hyperthermia
- Thirst
- Hunger
- Fatigue
- Loneliness
- Pain of Pride & Ego

All of the Seven Sisters, either alone or in cooperation with one another, contribute towards panic. Panic leads to despair. Despair invites more Sisters until ultimately, the individual loses their will to be a survivor and instead becomes a victim. Keeping a positive attitude about one's situation, combined with a sound foundation of knowledge and skill, will do much towards fending off the Sisters and their attempts at undermining your survival efforts. Keeping busy, working to improve your situation – no matter how slight an improvement – can have a powerful effect on staving off panic.

Staying focused on the tasks at hand will do much to keep your mind from succumbing to the 7 Sisters. Have a plan. Plan to survive. Execute your plan when you need to.

The Seven Sisters play into one another and work in unison to promote death. A mind clouded by fear may not remember to do something, even something basic. Severe thirst, hunger, fatigue and hypo/hyperthermia can all impair your ability to think clearly, remain calm and focus on making it through an ordeal. Also, ego and pride can be powerful detriments to survival. "I'm not going to signal for help, I've got this under control." or, "I'm an experienced hiker/soldier/woods-person/general bad-ass – I can get out of this." This type of individual is at a high risk of failure to survive. They falsely believe that they are superior and fail to recognize the extent of a bad situation. Their egos cannot accept compromising for safety and, consequently, they end up making their situation worse. Examples of this would be: not preparing for the outing properly, getting caught in poor weather and pushing on instead of stopping, believing they can find their way if lost, etc. These are all bad situations made worse by making poor decisions based on pride or ego. Forget your ego. Forget your pride. Mother Nature doesn't care what race, sex, creed, religion, etc. you are. She is an equal-opportunity killer.. You'll die just the same. Do the smart thing. Survive! How does this relate to being prepared in a disaster? It directly correlates because if the machinations of comfortable urban life are suddenly taken away (heat, water, food, shelter, fire and electricity on demand), then you are no longer safe, you are at risk of harm. You are at the mercy of the elements and possibly other people desperate because they are in the same boat. So, in order to maintain those things necessary to our survival, we must prepare for those things to be taken away.

DISASTER PLANNING

Why do we plan? Every day, people live with the risk of experiencing an unplanned for event which will threaten their safety. Depending on the nature of the event, especially in an urban context, you may choose to stay in-place to ride out the event or, alternatively, you may decide it is better to remove yourself from the affected area and grind through from another more stable location. The same applies to you if you are traveling. Depending on the nature of the event, you may decide to stay or move. This is all dependent on the individual variables in play at the time. Personal, medical, and family emergencies are often more complex to deal with overseas, as are political and civil unrest scenarios, not to mention natural disasters.

Managing these incidents involves the "detect, deter, response, recovery" model to identify, assess, and respond appropriately to emerging threat events. When in an urban/suburban environment, the resources needed to adequately prepare for such events may be available beforehand, but can also be quickly depleted once the event has initiated and the masses have begun to panic. This is exactly why being prepared with prepositioned supplies and knowledge is of paramount importance to giving yourself the best chance possible of making it through.

Don't make the mistake of thinking that it can't happen to you.

"But what if nothing happens? What if I never need to use this stuff?" That's a common and not insignificant question. It's in fact, very valid. So what if nothing happens? Then that's good. But let's consider a few points with that. Do you own ANY insurance policies? Life, mortgage, auto, home, chronic illness, travel, kidnap? If the answer is yes to any of those, ask yourself why? Sometimes, it's because the government mandates that you must have it. But for those that are elective, why? It's in case something happens. It's a safety net of your own design. Getting organized is a good thing. Getting fit is a good thing. Having a back-up in case something happens is a good thing. Having a disaster preparedness plan and directed supplies are you insurance for when something unexpected happens which you have no control over and your efforts pay you back in safety, security, comfort and piece-of-mind. THAT'S why I advocate investing some time and money to implement a preparedness plan. It's insurance, plain and simple.

The 7 Ps. The 7 Ps have their origins in the military world. *Proper Previous Planning Prevents Piss-Poor Performance.* Very simple and very true.

Take any scenario, assume the worst possible outcomes – really, let your imagination go wild – and then assess which of those outcomes you feel are necessary to plan for, and plan for those.

Planning in this context is called Risk Management. The basic principles of risk management are the identification of Hazards (things that are possible) and the Probability of those things happening (how likely is it to happen). The combination of those two (what is possible to happen, combined with their likelihood of happening) equals the level of RISK. When you have looked at your situation through risk-coloured glasses, you will be better equipped to gauge your level of RISK to a certain situation and plan accordingly.

When planning for disasters and emergencies, consider your specific situation and geographical area. Urban, sub-urban, rural, remote? Climatic conditions in your area. Are you close to flood-prone bodies of water or on flood-planes? Is your area at risk for wildfires? Droughts? Earthquakes? Tornadoes? Hurricanes? Winter storms? Are you in an unstable political or social landscape? Are the necessities of life dependent on supplies being trucked-in or dependent on the electrical grid? Are you in a condo or apartment/house/row-house/complex/suburb? What resources do you have available to you? What level of preparedness do you want to reach, and to mitigate what risks?

Consider the following list of possible threats and hazards you may be faced with:

- Flood
- Earthquake
- Snow Storm / Ice storm / deep freeze
- Tornado
- Hurricane/typhoon
- Civil Unrest / Riots / Violent demonstrations (breakdown in law and order)
- Martial Law (controls & restricts movements of people and goods, suspension of liberties and due process)
- Thunderstorms / hail storms / Lightning strikes
- Heat wave
- Wildfires / forest fires
- Drought
- Volcanic eruption
- Landslides
- Tsunami/tidal wave

- Avalanche
- Home Invasion
- Pandemic / biological agent release
- Blackout / Power outage
- Hazardous materials spill
- Air pollution
- Water supply contamination
- Radioactive material release
- Chemical release (accidental or intentional)
- Food supply contamination / disruption
- Fire/wildfire (affecting your home, neighbourhood, city)
- Terrorist Attack / Bombing / Active shooter
- War / Military Attack
- Biochemical attack
- Riots, violent demonstrations or civil unrest
- Sinkhole
- Solar storms / solar flare
- Economic collapse
- EMP (Electro-magnetic pulse)
- Airplane/Train/Ship/Truck crash/Derailment
- Zombies? Alien invasion? Clowns?

Now, not all of the above may be hazards in your area or in your particular situation. However, they do provide a reasonable cross-section of the threats you should be considering when beginning to prepare to face them.

Take into account the other various factors which may positively or negatively affect your situation. Are there any sources of water nearby? Is there a park or wooded area near you? Do you live in a condo building or perhaps a townhouse with a small yard? Are you on the coast? Near woodlands? Fault lines? Are you in a valley? Are you close to urban centers where repair and rescue crews can reach you easily, or are you isolated and remote in the suburbs? Desert? Near lakes/rivers? How many people are in your planned party? Are you planning for just yourself? Your spouse? Children? Pets? Elderly, pregnant, or very young? Special needs or conditions which require specialized preparations to ensure survivability? Do you live in a high-crime area or an area flirting with social breakdown? Are you living close to an international border? Identify other possible hazards in your are or that may affect you. Look for concentrations of graffiti or gang activity; streets, roads or intersections that are regularly congested; railroad tracks; nearby chemical plants, refineries & fuel storage depots; other threats or potential dangers in your area. All of these things have the ability to affect you or not, depending on the type of disaster you may be facing. You best consider the possibilities and prepare for the worst accordingly.

All of the above are part of your planning phase. Consider the specific disaster or circumstance you or your family may find yourselves in. Think back. What has happened in your area before? Do you recall? If you're new to the area, ask a long-time resident. Do some online research. Check the news. Be aware of the local, regional and national news sources (such as radio stations and television channels which provide emergency information for your area. Pay attention to weather patterns and warnings for your area. Be familiar with the hazards that exist. Find the worst and prepare to be able to deal with that situation with relative comfort for two hundred hours (200hrs, just over a week).

A good place to start is by asking at your workplace about what emergency protocols there may be in place. Simple things such as telework arrangements or call-in work to mitigate hazardous travel may already be in place. You can also ask about any emergency notification protocols that exist, such as a call-out list. By the same token, check in with other appropriate institutions, such as child care center or schools, for their applicable protocols so that you are informed about what to expect in a given situation should it arise.

Generally speaking, governmental public safety guidelines speak to developing the means to be self-sufficient for up to 72 hrs during an emergency, as that is the likely minimum time limit that it would take for help to reach you. The question you want to ask yourself is: "do I just want to squeak by in that case, or be okay through such an ordeal"? I propose you aim for being prepared to a minimum of 200hrs or at least a week. When the rest of the populace is scraping the bottom of their 72 hr plan, you should still be fine.

"Event Timeline":

- **0-24hrs** – Social co-operation and altruistic assistance
- **24-72hrs** – Social conventions begin to break down and suspicion grows as people start looking out for their own needs;
- **72-120hrs+** - Everyone for themselves. Almost no Rule of Law. Desperation, violence, greed, revenge and chaos until order is restored.

Part of being prepared is having the flexibility and adaptability to deal with unforeseen variables respecting your plan. A 72 hr plan may work fine if set up for yourself and your family – but what happens if disaster strikes and your mother-in-law happens to be there? I know what I'd do (ha ha ha!), but for some others, you might consider keeping them in your home. But now you have another mouth to feed for three days. Is that something you planned for? If you planned for doing well for 200 hrs, but have an extra couple of people, then you'll still be ahead of the game for the 72 hr window. Either way, you're ahead. Also, do consider a secondary disaster or event or a compromise of some of your supplies. What if vermin destroy some of your stored food? Or moisture? By planning for the upper edge of 200 hrs you will ultimately be more solvent to make it through that 72 hr window. Government websites and preparedness guides suggest 72 hours. Go above and beyond what others are doing. To do this, create an Emergency Plan.

Having an emergency plan gives you a framework to work with so that in the event of a real emergency, you will already know what to do. Part of the development process is to discuss the goals, expectations and desired outcomes for those subject to the emergency plan.

Let's go over some steps on how to create an actionable Emergency Disaster Readiness Plan.

1. Make an assessment of the likely disasters that may affect you.
2. Approach your local Fire Department or municipal emergency planning office and ask about the local hazards they prepare for and what they recommend are likely hazards to affect your area.
3. Learn what local radio stations provide emergency information during an event. Some jurisdictions operate cellular phone messaging/SMS alerts you can sign up for to receive timely updates.
4. Assess the individual needs of those for whom you are planning and

These goals, expectations and desired outcomes should bear on all affected members of the group, what everyone's roles are given an emergency situation and what the final resolution should be in an ideal state, as well as in redundancy.

Develop a loose but reliable network (if possible) of people (family, close friends and/or trusted neighbours) both close to you and out of your town and regional area which can act as contact points in the aftermath of a disaster. This would give you someone to leverage resources for you and provide logistics support and mutual aid and also communications from afar to help you out. They would be the ones with whom you would check in to let them know you're ok and what your status is. They may also be the ones to where you may evacuate to if things get bad enough.

This mirrors one of the goals, expectations and desired outcomes for planning: the designation of meeting or assembly points for the appropriate disaster, such as:

- Across the street in the event of a house fire;
- Somewhere in another part of town if things in your neighbourhood are unmanageable;
- An out-of-town alternate location in the event of a large-scale, regional disaster prompting evacuation. Ensure that all members of the party are aware of the designated location and have means to get there, as well as having a signal to make their way their.
- My Home is My Castle – if the situation calls for staying put, then fortification and organization of your home becomes a priority.

As the saying goes, get your house in order first. Ensure your home is as safe and secure as it can be. Ensure you have as many safety features build in to your home and in place for immediate use and that you can use it to sustain yourself.

Next, we will look at creating a Disaster Plan.

This begins with collating and organizing the information above. Once that is done and the information has been reviewed and priorities set and hazards identified, discussing these with your group (be it your family or chosen partners) and deciding on a plan of action should these occur is the next step. You will want to determine what the "tripwire" is for initiating your preparedness plan. Under what circumstances does the plan get activated, and how is that communicated to all members of the group? Discuss what to do in the event of an evacuation, including protocols for those with special requirements and pets if applicable. This must be understood by all and regularly confirmed and practiced to ensure readiness. Depending on the scale of the event, everyone should be familiar with Primary, Secondary and Tertiary meeting spots, progressively away from your home base. For instance, Primary could be down the block, Secondary, across town, and Tertiary, out of town beyond the geographical reach of the event.

To make sure you are prepared to initiate your plan, ensure all members of your family (or group) know the plan and are aware of their responsibilities.

Here are some examples:

- Ensure your home is in good repair – roof, foundation, windows, doors, utility systems, and that all family members have the knowledge and ability to shut down utilities (such as water, electricity and gas).
- Have quality, functional and tested smoke and carbon monoxide detectors in key places;
- Station appropriate fire extinguishers in your home (ABC-type);
- Make sure your home is insured against appropriate hazards and risks;
- Have important and emergency phone numbers posted beside all phones and in a known accessible location and ensure all family members are able to call for help if needed;
- Assemble and station your emergency supplies and emergency preparedness kit in a known location to all;

- Know the locations of and means to shut off electricity, gas and water to the house and ensure all members of your family or group know as well;
- Try to get everyone over twelve years old first aid and CPR training;
- Institute a "safe word" for the immediate members of your family. In the event of an emergency, the safe word would be given to an acquaintance or even stranger to identify the person as "safe" to the other family member so that they can verify authenticity and security. It can also be used over the phone. It is ONLY to be given in dire emergency. Similarly, you can implement a "danger" word which would tip off another person in the know that there is duress and to help. These types of code words would be taught to your kids to prevent a stranger from goading them into following them after saying "Your Mom/Dad was in a car accident and I'm supposed to come get you" and abduct them. The child should provide a challenge and expect the correct code word. If it is not delivered, they should make noise, run, shout, scream, find help and otherwise get away as this is clearly an imposter.
- Check your house for commonly accessible hazards. Look for and secure medicines, toxins, poisons and flammable products and secure them from children and pets or from possible compromise by leaks or accidental mixing. Keep liquids low and solids/powers higher up.
- If you happen to live in **an apartment or condo**, understand the limits of your space but also what resources are available to you. Do you have a balcony you can rig-up to collect rainwater? To grow a container garden on? For ventilation? What access do you have to power/plumbing/utilities? Can you still access the stairs in an emergency? Is there a water feature within

reasonable walking distance (to collect water for use after purification)? What is your sun exposure, so as to plan when your space gets light and heat? These factors, in conjunction with the overarching preparedness plan and storage of supplies (either in the apartment or in a storage locker if you have one) is to be taken into consideration. You can also consider partnering with a neighbour towards a team approach.

Common Disaster Types and Preparations for Them

Not all "disasters" are the catastrophes of the scale depicted in Hollywood films, like an Earth-ending asteroid. Something as "simple" as a kitchen fire can turn deadly and disastrous should it quickly get out of control and engulf the entire house. Let's go over some of the more common disasters (or 'events') that the average person can be affected by and what you can do to prepare to mitigate their impact.

Power Outages:

- These are very common and can range from lasting minutes and be of minor irritation, to lasting more than a week and, depending on the season and weather, be quite impactful. This loss of power can compromise heating, cooling, water, sanitation, lighting, communications and security.
- Pre-pack a "black-out box" or have your home preparedness kit include power-redundancies. These include flashlights and spare batteries, solar or battery-powered radio, glow sticks, candles & lighters and a few back-up battery banks. If using candles, do not leave them unattended and make sure they are placed in fire-proof containers.

- If your heat and cooking sources are electric, set up an alternative with extra fuel.
- Consider investing in a back-up generator and spare fuel to meet critical needs for power if needed. Another option if you have natural gas, is to get an in-line gas-powered back-up generator which will power your home with natural gas should the power go out. Natural gas will continue to flow through the lines even without power in all but the most dire of circumstances.
- During a power outage, check to see if yours is the only house without electricity or if others are also affected. Depending on the weather, you may want to walk around the neighbourhood and see how far the outage reaches. If yours is the only house without power, you may want to call the utility company and check your breakers/fuses. If the outage is due to downed power lines, contact the electrical utility company and/or fire department as soon as possible and avoid the area to remain safe.
- If the outage continues for a while, consider unplugging or turning off large or sensitive electronics and higher-wattage appliances to avoid damage until regular power is restored.
- Be conservative with your water, as your pump may not work without power (especially if you are on a well).
- Only open your fridge when needed to maintain temperature.
- If you plan on using gas-powered heaters or lanterns or BBQs, that you have adequate ventilation and working battery-powered carbon monoxide detectors to avoid death from poison fumes.
- Once the power is restored, reset your breaker system and one-by-one, go through the house and turn on all the electronics you turned off or disconnected previously. Check on the food in your fridge and freezer for spoilage.

- Tip: leave a lamp or light switch in the "on" position to alert you to when power is restored.

Fires:

- Millions of residential fires occur every year. It is one of the most likely disasters for those living in an urban or suburban environment to experience. House fires can spread quickly and overpower residents through smoke and toxic gas inhalation. Protecting your home from fires can be done straight-forwardly and effectively with some planning and regular maintenance.
- Invest in quality smoke and carbon-monoxide detectors, installed on every floor and near appliances capable of combustion (like a clothes dryer, furnace, gas hot water heater, fireplace (gas or wood) or boiler. Ideally, they should be wired together through the house with battery back-ups and tested monthly.
- Purchase appropriate fire extinguishers for the home (ABC-type) and ensure all members of your family know how to use them. Make sure they are charged and still within their valid dates. If needed, get them inspected and re-charged.
- In the event of discovering a fire, take appropriate measures to extinguish it IF it is small and generally contained. Do not use precious time to fight a fire if failure to successfully extinguish it may result in you or others being trapped. Use those precious seconds to get out safely and then call 911.

- If you or someone else catches fire, STOP-DROP-ROLL and try to smother the fire with a blanket or something fire-retardant.
- If you have a grease fire, try to extinguish it by covering the pot with a lid, or by using baking soda or salt to smother it. If that doesn't work, fire extinguisher. DO NOT use water.
- DO NOT USE WATER on an electrical fire – use a fire extinguisher!
- If you detect a fire, check the door for heat and smoke before opening it. If the handle is hot, don't open the door. Seek an alternate exit. If smoke is entering the room under the door, use towels, blankets etc (wet if possible) to stuff in the gap.
- Ensure all members of your family know exits from the house, what the evacuation plan is and where to assemble should a fire occur. Evacuation should be the top priority in the event of a fire.

Winter Storms (Snow, Ice, Deep freeze):

- Winter storms can cover entire geographic regions for days and even weeks at a time. This can be through a combination of extreme precipitation, extremely low temperatures, heavy snow, high winds, sleet, ice and freezing rain. This can impact transportation routes and logistical supplies (blocked or hazardous roads affecting food, fuel and materiel deliveries while making travel dangerous and slow.) while simultaneously knocking out power and isolating residents. Winter storms can, in the worst cases, be a catalyst for a terrible situation.
- Prepare for winter storms by being forewarned and aware. Listen to alerts and warnings on the local news and prepare accordingly. If you plan to leave the area, do so BEFORE the storm hits. If you plan to stay, implement aspects of your

disaster plan into a "standby" pattern and either increase or decrease as needed.
- Ensure you have adequate food and means to cook it.
- Fuel your car and station extra fuel if needed.
- If you live in an area prone to winter storms, GET SNOW TIRES and install them in the Fall BEFORE winter hits. Swap them out in the Spring for your "all seasons". (I usually switch mine around Canadian Thanksgiving and Easter). If you must travel, consider using public transit (if it's running) and lower the risk of your own vehicle being damaged and you being injured. And drive according to conditions.
- Have a supply of ice melter, along with quality snow shovels, scrapers, etc.
- Anticipate the need to upgrade your status to "power outage" at some point. Ice storms typically knock out power due to downed power lines.
- When shoveling snow, take regular breaks and don't overdo it. It is very common for people to have heart attacks while shoveling snow due to the level of stress this activity causes the body. Wear layers. Ventilate, vent sweat and stay hydrated as dehydration can happen quickly during periods of intense activity in dry, cold environments.
- Be aware of the effects of cold on the body, including frostbite and hypothermia.

Floods:

- Floods are another common disaster faced by many people who live in flood plains and near rivers, lakes and oceans. These bodies of water can swell due to weather systems and seasonal

changes (such as spring melts and runoff) and be dictated in some way by the geography, both natural and man-made.
- In cities, flooding most often occurs when heavy rains and runoff overwhelms sewer systems and water backs up into basements or overflows and floods streets. Depending on where you are situated, there may be little you can do to divert urban floods.
- To prevent back-flows, consider installing back-up/back-flow valves which will prevent sewers from backing up into your home. Sewer backups usually bring with them raw sewage and can cause costly damage to your basement and its contents.
- Those living on high ground or in apartments and condos are less likely to be directly affected by flooding, however, urban flooding can cause power transformers to become flooded resulting in power outages. If water mains are damaged, potable water supplies may become interrupted or compromised as utility crews work to restore service.
- If you live in an urban area near dams, levees and in flood plains should identify these and plan accordingly. Buy flood insurance if ANY of these apply to you and be sure you're covered if your home is flooded out. In the Ottawa River Valley floods of 2019, many residents were refused insurance payouts because they lived in a "known" (to the insurance companies) flood plain and had not purchased additional flood riders on their policies.
- If you are in a flood-prone area, pre-position supplies to defend your home with (sand bags, shovels, sand, plastic sheeting, pumps, etc) and check in with your local emergency management office to understand their response plans for your area. Ask them for local maps and plans identifying urban waterways, underground streams and rivers as well as overflow

- Be prepared to evacuate the area and consider keeping several tough, air-tight containers (such as Nanuk, Pelican, etc.) to store important personal items which you may not be able to take with you and store in the upper levels of your house upon evacuation to ensure their safety.
- Pay attention to local weather reports. If there are flood warnings, stay away from waterways as their volume and speed can be deceptively dangerous and sweep away people, vehicles and even houses (I've seen it).
- Stay away from flood-affected areas if possible and be aware that all flood waters are likely contaminated and you should wash & decontaminate yourself and clothing. Wash your hands regularly.
- Consider all your non-bottled water as contaminated. Boil and purify as required. If possible, fill up your bathtub (clean it first) and make yourself a reservoir of water you can access for sterilization and drinking. You can also use a WaterBob to line your tub and contain the clean potable water for later use.

Earthquakes:

- Earthquakes are high risk for some, but some risk to all. You likely already know if you live in an urban area in a earthquake-prone zone or along a fault line. If you don't know, find out. Earthquakes strike without warning and can be either minor irritations or catastrophic in scale. They can cause buildings to collapse, roads to come apart, tsunamis, fires, landslides and knock out utility services.
- If you are in an earthquake-prone area, consider upgrading your home/auto/article insurance to make sure it will cover you if the resultant damage is the result of an earthquake. Some policies

require additional riders and are not automatically part of your standard policy.
- Pre-position your preparedness kit in as accessible a method as possible to ensure easy access in the event of an earthquake.
- Identify safe places in your home and work environments in the event you have to take cover from falling debris if an earthquake starts. Identify escape routes to expedite movement to relative safety.
- Especially if you live on above-ground floors, the higher up the more you will feel the sway. Secure your belongings as if you are on a sailboat. Affix furniture to walls, install cabinet latches,

Survival Priorities and A Multi-Tiered Preparedness Strategy

To enable one to plan to prepare, one needs to understand what priorities they are preparing for and to what scale. When it comes to preparedness, you are the one who decides to what lengths you want to go, how necessary it is and how much time/money/training you are willing to invest. You can start with the most basic preparations and build on them over time. There is no need to rush out in a panic and spend yourself into debt just to feel safe. To effectively establish a preparedness framework you need to understand your priorities – the basics., then build from there.

TIP: *Remember redundancy – Two is one, one is none. If you have put all of your proverbial eggs in the basket of one item that your survival hinges on, then do yourself a favour and get a second one. Things break. It happens at the most inopportune times. So get a second one and thank yourself later.*

In the context of urban disasters these are as follows:

- Shelter
- Water
- Fire & Heat

- Food
- Medical & First Aid
- Sanitation & Health
- Communications
- Power and back-ups and;
- Security

The above are general guidelines insofar as they can be moved into a different order of importance dependent upon your specific situation. For instance, if you live in a high-rise with a stocked pantry, food and shelter may not be as important as water. You get the idea. Once your first four major priorities are taken care of, you would expand your preparations to include the secondary. If a member of your party is suffering from a grievous injury, the "first aid" priority goes straight to the top of the list. If they bleed out, all the water and fire in the world won't help.

To begin our preparatory inventory, you want to have the right approach. You get what you pay for. Invest wisely in quality items and training that you will have confidence in living up to their claims. This is potentially your life (and that of others) you're talking about. Preparedness isn't as much a "thing to do", rather its a life philosophy and way of being. An outlook. Making a habit of forethought will keep you ready to meet challenges head-on through ingrained flexibility. To achieve this, we develop our strategy from ourselves outward – in levels.

*EXAMPLES OF EACH LEVEL

Level 1. EDC (Every Day Carry)

Level 2. Personal Emergency Kit (Vehicle, Office desk, Briefcase)

Level 3. 1-Week Kit Home Disaster Preparedness / Evacuation kit (Bug-In Box (BIB) / Bug-Out Bag (BOB) good for 200+ hours.)

Level 4. Home Preparedness Kit (for survival in the home for beyond 1 week to 1 month +)

Level 5. Long Term Self-Sufficiency & Preparedness Lifestyle Strategy (beyond 1 month without re-supply, complete self-reliance)

In this book, we will be focusing on Levels 1 through 3. (Levels 4 & 5 require more in-depth planning and resources, as well as skills beyond the scope of this publication.)

Each Level should address the basic survival and preparedness priorities in an urban or suburban context. With each subsequent level, that equipment should be duplicated to ensure against failure. Remember, "two is one, one is none" (Old military adage). If you only have one "thing" and it breaks or fails on you, you have nothing. But if you have a back-up, you'll have a secondary when your primary fails. The types of equipment specific to each priority will be discussed in the following chapters. For now let's discuss the preparation strategy.

Let's begin with **Level 1, your EDC, or Every Day Carry.** This is the basic equipment that you carry with you at all times, anytime you leave the house. These should address the basics.

I carry the following as my Every Day Carry:

- Pocket knife (Swiss Army knife, low-profile) and ceramic razor blade.
- Bic Lighter
- Small flashlight & mini glow sticks
- Pen
- Lock picks / entry tools
- Emergency restraint escape tools (for self)

- Emergency Cash (enough to get food, some tools and transportations in a pinch)
- Cell phone & charging cable (with wall plug)
- Para-cord & Kevlar cordage
- Bare-bones first aid supplies (bandaids, Tylenol).

Consider the following: clothing appropriate for the weather (shelter), small lighter (fire), bottle of water (water), granola bar in your glove box, pocket or purse (food), first aid kit in car with wipes (first aid/sanitation), cell phone and car radio (communications), small flashlight on your keychain or in your glove-box (light), spare asthma vaporizer in glove box (special consideration). Also, a multi-tool and/or sharp pocket knife (either on you and/or duplicated in your vehicle/bag). Some form of cordage. Para-cord as shoe laces or a length or it in your vehicle – maybe a para-cord survival bracelet?

The above is a fairly comprehensive list for an EDC kit. The above would help someone with basic survival knowledge and training to be able to make it through a minor survival situation of short duration. Typically getting through the day to get you back home.

Make sure you have a knife or blade of some sort. Make sure it is sharp. Make sure it is quality. Sharp is safe, dull is dangerous As for options like fixed-blade or folding blade and serrated versus plain edge and grinds and tips, these are all personal preference and... .for you to determine according to your needs.

Always consider the "little things". Dehydration is a key consideration. If you think you have enough water to maintain you through an ordeal, you don't. Survival situations are straining and stressful. Most people are not accustomed to the hard labour and sustained exertion that goes hand-in-hand with a survival situation. Working in offices does not usually mimic fighting for your life. Hypothermia and Hyperthermia is warded off through hydration. **WATER IS KEY!**

For Level 2, your Personal Emergency Kit – PEK

Your clothing itself should be "mission specific" and appropriate for your local weather conditions and climate and season. For the average person, choose something quick-drying in either polyester or nylon, light, bug-proof, helps keep a rash off you. Also consider compression shorts to prevent your thighs from rubbing through damp or wet clothing which can cause a rash or rubbing.

Tip: While in Iraq, my friend Dan kept track of the water he consumed on an average day. In one day he drank 19 1.5L bottles of Evian. WOW! And he was still thirsty.

An Air Force pilot friend of mine commented to me once that you should always "dress to egress". If disaster strikes and you have to get out in a hurry, will wearing heels & nylons or a suit and loafers get you through a winter storm, or help you escape an active shooter event? Not likely. Wear serviceable and strong clothes and footwear. Nondescript is better than flashy style. If you think fashion is important, just remember you'll be the best dressed person at the morgue, if you're lucky.

This level can also be carried in your car or remain in your office desk drawer to double as a "Get Home Bag" (GHB) for a situation where you are away from home and your main preparedness setup but returning is difficult. (You can duplicate this as often as you like and preposition the GHBs in regular places you may find yourself so that you can access them at any time. One in your office, one in your car, one in your gym locker – it's up to you). This GHB should enable you to get through a day of traversing the city with only what you have to get you back home. This can include a change of clothes and appropriate footwear, some basic tools, some cash, food and water, a defensive weapon (or means to make one), first aid supplies and maybe a flashlight/headlamp, whistle, map and compass. This setup should be able to facilitate a safe return home (traversing the city) to your main supplies. I would strongly recommend that the container you choose for your GHB be a sturdy backpack of a nondescript colour and pattern. Steer away from anything "tactical" looking or attention-grabbing colours and designs. The idea is to blend into the background of your environment and not become a target for those without supplies looking to get supplies, from you!.

Level 3 is your 200 hour kit.

If you will be hunkering down at your home to wait out a bad storm or weather system drought, etc., (also known as "bugging-in" or "shelter-in-place"), then you can pre-position essential items in a large bin or duffel bag somewhere in your home and draw on pre-existing supplies from your house to supplement what is needed. You can call this your BIB (or Bug-In Bin). Items such as extra blankets and clothing, food, water containers and tools are all likely available to you in your home and can be used with relative ease to stand up your disaster plan. You should still have your Level 1 and 2 kits on your person and in your vehicle but your Level 3, which is ultimately the backbone of what will be sustaining you for the 72-100/200hrs can be loosely organized through your home with only specialized or key "emergency-only" items set aside for dedicated use. These items should also regularly checked, maintained and cycled through to ensure reliable operation and freshness. You should also be practicing with the items you have for emergencies as if you are unfamiliar with them, a crisis is not the time to learn under pressure.

Heavy-duty totes, such as these pictured above from Home Depot, come in a few sizes, are durable and inexpensive. They do a great job of organizing your preparedness supplies in one easy-to-transport package if you have to transition from bug-in to bug-out.

If you needed to evacuate your home or "bug out", this would also be referred to as your "bug-out bag", "bug-out bin", or BOB. This is the goal to which you are striving. To achieve self-sufficiency during a disaster which threatens your life and being able to persevere through it with proper preparation and knowledge. You should be able to live out of your 200-hr kit or BOB should a disaster occur. Your BOB should be a self-contained, all-in-one package which is ready at a moments notice to be brought into operation. That is not to say that it should be shrink-wrapped and never be touched. You can use it for camping or hiking (if that's your thing), or to deal with every day life should its contents be required. Also, a BOB or 200-hr kit is a "living document" so to speak. It should always be updated, improved upon and reevaluated for effectiveness and efficiency. Let me reiterate: you should be able to weather any catastrophe for at least 72-200 hrs with only what you have in your Level 3 kit or BOB.

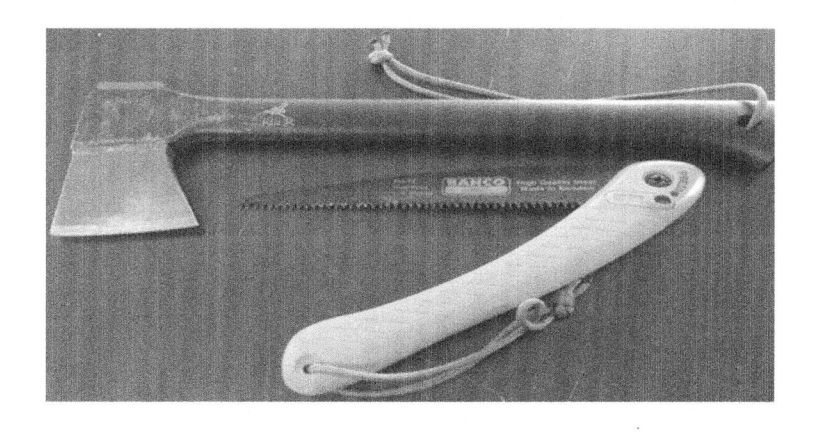

Having an axe and saw (see picture) can give you options.

Your 200hr kit should contain everything contained in your PSK, scaled to the level of those the kit is designed to sustain. For instance, if you are a family of four, then your kit should contain four multi-tools or knives, four flashlights with batteries, four lighters, a first-aid kit for 4, water & food for 4 for 200 hrs, heating and cooking options for four for 200hrs. etc... If you are a couple you can scale it down appropriately or up as you see fit, especially if you plan on taking others in during such a time of need.

This methodology should be framed in the context of the "Rule of 3s", which states the following (generally) to be true: You will die in...

3 minutes without air;

3 hrs without shelter (from exposure without heat);

3 days without water;

3 weeks without food;

These "Rules" are generally accepted guidelines in what one needs to survive. You should consider them accordingly in your preparation plan.

Which brings us to our next topic...

SHELTER

In the wilderness, animals either carry their shelter with them, have a natural instinct to create their own or a combination of both.

Humans have neither. We do, however, have the cognitive abilities to create for ourselves what Nature has given to the animal world.

In camping, hiking and wilderness survival, shelters range from tents, cabins, caves to brush shelters or a lean-to and the clothes on one's back. In an emergency preparedness interpretation of this, we are going to focus on shelter as what we wear, our dwelling and the augmenting with supplies that are at hand or that can be purchased.

First, the clothes you wear as shelter. Almost every day we wake up and get dressed in preparation to venture outside our homes. What we wear is directly affected by the environment in which we are venturing. For instance, you wouldn't wear a heavy down-filled parka during a heat wave, nor would you wear a swimsuit during a blizzard. You 'shelter' yourself accordingly, albeit with some level of style (one would think). Your choices in owning clothing in respect to preparing for a disaster should follow simple guidelines to ensure that your body is able to maintain optimal functioning temperature through thermoregulation. Thermoregulation is the body's way of producing or shedding heat in an effort to maintain an optimal core body temperature of 98.6 degrees.

With too little heat, one will develop hypothermia (being too cold). Eventually, if the body temperature drops too low, death will result. Conversely, if one's body temperature gets too high (hyperthermia), this too can lead to death. The clothes you wear (or don't) should enhance the body's ability to thermo-regulate, either by keeping heat in, or allowing heat out.

There are various ways that one gains and loses heat. They are as follows:

Conduction

(the transfer of heat (energy) through direct contact with an object, including hot or cold air, against the skin).

Convection

(the transfer of heat (energy) through currents in air and liquids and can be either forced or natural).

Evaporation

(the process of losing heat (energy) through the conversion of a liquid to a gas.

Radiation

(losing or gaining heat (energy) through long or short-wave radiation. Shortwave is from the Sun, long wave radiation is usually from things like fire, the human body or any other traditional heat source. And;

Respiration

(losing heat (energy) and water vapor through respiratory surfaces of the lungs by breathing).

If you live in an area which tends to be too hot on average, keeping cool will be your priority. Shade, breeze and being below ground, along with shedding layers of clothing and staying hydrated, will help towards keeping your core body temperature from getting dangerously high.

If however, your concern will be staying warm, you will have on-going challenges. When it comes to wearing your shelter to keep the cold at bay, remember the following acronym:

COLD:

C – keep yourself and your clothes CLEAN;

O – avoid OVERHEATING. You sweat, you die.;

L – wear clothes LOOSE and in LAYERS;

D – keep DRY.

Keeping the preceding in mind, ensure you wear appropriate clothing for the environment. When preparing for the unexpected, look to have spare clothes for every member of your group. These should ideally be natural or synthetic fibers (wool and fleece) which will maximize insulation. Avoid cotton as it becomes useless when wet or soiled. Additionally, down is the best insulator you can have as long as it remains DRY. It is useless when wet. If you are confidant that you can keep down functional, fill your boots on it.

For most people wanting to be prepared without going to extremes, there is no need to have to go out and buy extravagant items. Things that most people have can be used for more than one purpose. Having extra wool blankets or down duvets in one's linen closet are usually sufficient. Also, using the sleeping bags from your camping gear easily double as your emergency gear. If you only own summertime sleeping bags, consider putting one inside another for added warmth, rather than spending more on a "better" model. Having spare wool blankets is common for people to have around a house. In case of guests staying over unexpectedly or maybe wanting that bit of extra warmth when on the couch watching a movie. No one says that it can't be aesthetically pleasing. Just be mindful when arranging your linens or buying new ones, or if you happen to see something on sale someplace.

Other items which will aid in keeping you warm within your home can include:

- Sleeping bags (cocoon of warmth, use two if needed);
- Wool blankets (will help retain heat even when wet);
- closed-cell foam under-pads (to increase insulation from the cold floor);
- Tent (shelter within a shelter – smaller space to keep warm);
- Chemical heating pads (instant warmth);
- Extra clothing (wool, fleece & down);
- Space blankets (to reflect heat);

(An inexpensive sleeping bag added to your supplies can add a life-saving layer of warmth in the event of a winter power outage)

If the opposite is true and you find yourself in a situation where you are suffering from extreme heat, consider the following to help stay cool:

- Run your air conditioner if possible;
- Open windows, create a draft to move air through your home;
- Take wet towels and hang them at your windows – the draft will carry colder air as the water soaked in the towels evaporates;
- Wear loose-fitting, light coloured clothing made from thin and breathable materials;
- Choose natural materials like cotton over nylon, wear hats, sunglasses and light, long-sleeved shirts to prevent sunburn;
- Stay as hydrated as you can and ensure you are taking in electrolytes to replace those lost through sweating;
- Reduce activity during the mid-day hours when the sun and temperature are at their hottest;
- Create shade wherever you can. Keep exposed skin safe from prolonged sun exposure to reduce the possibility of sunburns which can be debilitating.

Once you have the clothes on your back, its time to move outwards, like with our other multi-tiered preparations. Next, we are going to look at our dwellings as a form of shelter, which is what they are. Homes are designed to keep us shielded from the elements. They are designed to be insulated from excessive cold or heat, wind, precipitation in all its manifestations. You home also keeps you safe from predators and pests while giving you a place to sleep in comfort, store your goods and enjoy yourself.

These principles are inherent in almost all human dwellings. Their level of resilience, however, varies. You will need to apply the same assessment strategy to your home or dwelling as you would for your overall preparedness plan. How is your home built? Is it sturdy? Where is it situated? Are there any built-in redundancies in its design? Is it secure from compromise by various threats? Is it prone to flooding? Is it protected from wind or storms by natural or man-made barriers? In the event of extreme weather you want your home to be able to provide you the most protection from the elements and other hazards as possible. For example, your home will be of little use in a winter storm if your insulation is ineffective and your windows have gaps which allow drafts. An efficiency assessment of home inspection would be able to give you a good idea as to where the areas for improvement are and how they can be addressed and mitigated.

To protect yourself and your family in a shelter-in-place scenario, you would want to ensure that, in addition to the roof, walls and foundation that protects you, that you integrate redundancy measures to compensate for the loss of the other survival priorities which your home usually provides but are easily compromised. A wood-burning fireplace of stove, for instance, provides heat for the house during good times and bad. With a supply of firewood on hand for several days and you won't freeze.

Such as, our next survival priority...

Minimum Suggestion: Have an extra sleeping bag or blanket for each member of your family/group.

FIRE, HEATING & COOKING

Most everyone's homes have in them some form of heating source (furnace or wood stove) and method of heating and preparing food (stove). These are sometimes one and the same, however, most modern homes have separate appliances for each function. These are most often powered by either electricity, fuel, or a combination of both. If your ability to heat your home, boil water and cook food is compromised, your ability to hold disaster at bay becomes severely compromised. Electrical power outages are fairly common. Even throughout the developed world, not to mention developing nations. The same goes for fuel heating. Natural gas lines can rupture. Propane of fuel oil tanks can run empty and not be resupplied during a disaster. Electricity is only as reliable as the strength of a tree branch during a storm. You MUST consider redundancies to maintain your ability to create heat and cook should your primary means of doing so is no longer viable. This needs not be elaborate or even expensive, but it MUST be safe, effective and reasonable for your situation.

First, look at your preparedness assessment and as yourself the following: "if the stove and furnace stop, how will I stay warm and boil water/cook food for a week"
?

If you live in a home with a fireplace, you only need ensure that you have a supply of firewood at hand and you can make it through. If you're a condo dweller, you might be looking at a propane heater and a camp stove. Camping equipment can usually do double duty in these situations, as long as there is sufficient fuel for the task. Having a back yard helps as well. Some people have finite storage space for firewood. Sometimes the better way to go might be a propane tank with 2-burner stove and small heater attachment with rationed use to last through the ordeal. Look at what you will need and plan accordingly.

(Having a working wood or gas-burning fireplace can be a game-changing element to a disaster situation)

There are a plethora of options for making fire in your home. The best option you would have is a wood stove or fireplace. Propane and kerosene heaters are also very viable options. If you have a BBQ at your home, acquire a few extra propane tanks and keep them filled in case you need to attach them to heaters or stoves. Once you have chosen a method(s) that you have the means to get them started at will and keep them going according to your needs. Fires don't just provide you with heat and the means of boiling water and cooking food, it also provides a positive psychological boost in times of need.

(Having a duel-fuel camp stove such as this Coleman model gives you a reliable stove alternative during a disaster)

DANGER: WHEN USING ANYTHING WHICH HEATS THROUGH COMBUSTION, ENSURE PROPER VENTILATION TO PREVENT CARBON MONOXIDE POISONING

Ensure you have working smoke and carbon monoxide detectors placed throughout your home, that they have fresh batteries and that they are regularly tested. Your life may depend on it.

Dual Smoke & Carbon Monoxide detectors are ideal as life safety devices in all living spaces and they stay active during power outages to warn you of problems. Get them, keep fresh batteries and test them regularly.

Here is a list of fire-related options:

- strike-anywhere matches
- lighter (Bic, zippo, etc.)
- Flint striker
- Tinder (cotton balls & petroleum jelly, birch bark, commercial fire starter)
- WOOD! (with saw and axe to split it)
- Steel wool and batteries
- BBQ lighter
- Candles (beeswax burns hotter and longer, is natural and smells nice)
- Magnifying glass/Fresnel lens
- Propane canisters

- Kerosene
- Camp fuel for stoves & heaters (aka White Gas)
- Lamp oil / kerosene
- Sterno fondue fuel-gel cans
- Chemical heating pads / MRE cooker packs

A selection of fire starting implements (above) should always be on hand in case of emergency.

Everyone preparing for a disaster should at LEAST have the first four items on the above list. Keeping most of the items in your home is easy, inexpensive and provides great peace of mind. Ensure you know how to use everything and try it out one day and see how it goes. Give it a dry run.

Having a small stick stove (like this stainless steel KIHD Stove) can at least boil a pot of water for you no matter the circumstances – and it folds flat.

To increase the efficiency of your heat sources, try to use your cooking heat to do double duty and heat the area you will be spending most of your time. Maybe move the entire group to one larger room and cook and sleep there. Seal up the windows with duct tape and plastic sheeting to seal out drafts. Use the shiny side of aluminum foil to create a heat and light reflector around candles and lanterns. Try lining the walls with space blankets to reflect the heat and light around the room and increase efficiency and combine everyone's body heat to add to the ambient temperature. Even a few degrees can mean the difference between living and dying should the situation be so dire. Also, consider sharing sleeping bags, or getting everyone under one big wool blanket.

Personal heaters, like these hot pocket-types, stay warm for hours and can be used to supplement your core body temperature and keep extremities from frostbite. They are small, inexpensive and effective.

A camp stove (above) paired with a few fuel canisters (below) can provide efficient cooking for a condo resident for a solid week.

43

Minimum Suggestion: A couple of disposable lighters, a box of candles, flashlight & spare batteries, small rocket stove or propane burner and fuel canister for 200 hrs. A pair of gel fuel chafing dish heaters (Sterno fuel) are good too.

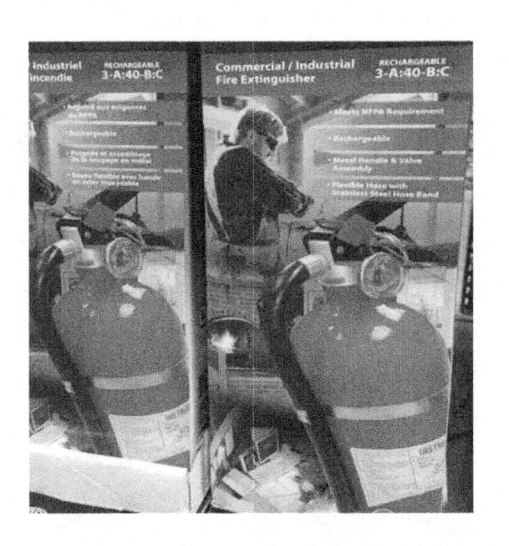

If you plan on burning anything, or using a stove or combustable fuel of any kind, ALWAYS have at least a pair of fire extinguishers in your living space. The A:B:C kinds are most versatile for residential use.

WATER

Without a doubt, if you don't have water for a few days, you're going to have a bad time. Your ability to stay hydrated must always remain a top-tier priority. Your goal for having water stored or readily available should be roughly:

2 gallons (7.5 – 8 Liters) per person, per day.

Enough non-potable water for at least one toilet flush per person, per day, for 14 days.

Rotating your stockpile every 6 months

Having a water safety test kit to ensure your methods are effective.

There are many sources of water around you. Sometimes looking with a different perspective will help a great deal. As there are many methods of acquiring water, in an emergency almost any source of water can be treated to be a viable source. These include:

- Wells (if available)
- Rain water (collected by catchment systems)
- Rivers, streams, creeks and other moving bodies of water
- Ponds and lakes
- Natural springs
- Melting snow or ice

- Collecting dew or rainwater
- Transpiration (securing large plastic bags over green foliage to trap the plant's perspiration)
- Solar still
- Water in your hot water tank (taken with proper precautions)
- Toilet tank (NOT THE BOWL!)
- Residual water in your home pipes
- Bottled water
- Previously stored water

There are many options for collecting, storing, filtering, treating or otherwise purifying water for safe consumption are many. After the tried and true boil, there are filters, chemical treatment methods and simple storage options available to suit all levels of preparedness and budget. For condo dwellers, storing a couple of cases of bottled water and a bathtub-sized water reservoir (brand name Water BOB) you should be just fine. Others may consider various other options.

These can include:

- Pots for boiling water
- Chlorine bleach drops
- Iodine drops
- Various water filters (Sawyer, LifeStraw, MSR, Big Berkey, Katadyn, LIFESAVER Systems, etc.)
- Desalination device (if living near seawater)
- Water BOB & siphon pump (to use in a bathtub)
- Rain barrel & catchment systems
- Bottled water & water tank storage systems
- Water purification tablets
- Active oxygen purification drops

- Water mats (Aquaflex Aqua tank – like a Water BOB but for under your bed)
- Water storage barrels (must have the #2 inside the recycle triangle on bottom)
- Stainless steel (or food grade plastic) storage tanks (best option if cost not an issue)
- Water Cubes (stack like lego)
- You can also look to instal in-line water treatment systems, such as O3 (Ozone) and UV (Ultraviolet) purifiers paired with sand filters and reverse-osmosis filters. These are typically standard in homes that are on wells in the country, however they are options to be installed within your existing plumbing and, depending on their size and complexity, can be inexpensive and very effective.

A selection of personal-sized water filters include (L to R) Aquamira, LifeStraw and the Sawyer Mini. All

inexpensive, small and very effective, especially for an urban or apartment context.

Water is without a doubt a crucial element to your disaster preparedness plan. Fortunately, it need not be a difficult commodity to keep under control. With the proper preparation, one can ensure that various sources of water are safe to drink. An additional positive is that you can always add and improve your stockpile and collection & purification methods.

Why should you disinfect your drinking water?

Drinking water is disinfected to kill bacteria, viruses and parasites, which may be present and may cause illness and disease. Left untreated in extreme situations, this can also lead to death.

Many different diseases are spread by contaminated drinking water, including Campylobacter, cholera, amoebic dysentery, Giardia (beaver fever) and Cryptosporidia.

These organisms usually get into drinking water supplies when source waters such as lakes or streams, community water supply pipes, or storage reservoirs are contaminated by animal wastes or human sewage.

In general, surface waters such as lakes and streams are more likely to contain disease-causing organisms than groundwater, however groundwater is usually more likely to be contaminated by leeching toxins and heavy metals. Deep wells are usually safer than shallow wells. In fact, shallow dug wells are often as contaminated as lakes or streams.

When should you disinfect/treat your drinking water?

You should disinfect your drinking water if:

- Your community is subject to a boil water advisory;
- You are using water directly from a stream, lake or shallow well;
- Lab tests of your water show that it contains "fecal coliforms";
- A flood, earthquake or other disaster has disrupted your community water supply;
- You are traveling in an area where water is not well treated; or
- You have a weakened immune system, in which case you should disinfect all of your drinking water.

Disinfecting small amounts of water:

Boiling:

Boiling is the best way to kill bacteria, viruses and parasites. A full boil for at least one minute is recommended. At elevations over 2,000 meters (6,500 feet) you should boil water for at least two minutes to disinfect it. NOTE: This is not appropriate for water that is heavily polluted or subject to chemical or heavy metal contamination.

Disinfection using chemical methods:

Unscented household bleach with 5% chlorine can sometimes be a good disinfectant. For example, this may work when the water is not heavily polluted, or when Giardia or cryptosporidiosis are not a concern.

Bleach does not work well in killing off Giardia, 'beaver fever' or Cryptosporidium parasites. The amount of bleach needed to kill these parasites makes the water almost impossible to drink. If Cryptosporidium or Giardia are in your water, boiling is the best way to ensure safe drinking water.

Disinfection using bleach works best with warm water. Add 1 drop (0.05 mL) of bleach to 1 Liter of water, shake and allow to stand for at least 30 minutes before drinking. Double the amount of bleach for cloudy water or for cooler water. A slight chlorine odour should still be noticeable at the end of the 30-minute waiting period if you have added enough bleach. The longer the water is left to stand after adding bleach, the more effective the disinfection process will be.

Chlorine Tablets:

Follow the manufacturers' directions.

Iodine:

Whenever possible use warm water (20°C) and let stand a minimum of 20 minutes after mixing and before drinking. For cold water (5 – 15°C) increase the waiting time after mixing to 40 minutes. If you are using 2% tincture of iodine, use 10 drops (0.5 mL) for every one litre of water. With iodine tablets, follow the manufacturer's directions.

Note: *Pregnant women should not use iodine drops to purify water as it may have a negative effect on the fetus.*

Iodine should not be used to disinfect water over long periods of time as prolonged use can cause thyroid problems./p>

Disinfecting large amounts of water:

Always use clean containers designed for storage of food or water. You can use regular household bleach (usually about 5% chlorine) or commercial bleach products (usually 10% chlorine).

The table below shows how much regular household bleach to add to various size water containers to disinfect relatively clean water.

If you are treating water from a lake, stream or shallow well, use twice as much household (5%) bleach as indicated in the chart below and wait twice as long before drinking it because it is more likely to contain chlorine-resistant parasites from animal droppings.

Let the water stand for at least an hour after adding the bleach before you start drinking it. If the water is colder than 10°C or has a pH higher than 8, let the water stand for at least two hours before drinking.

Gallons of water to disinfect (equivalent shown in brackets)	Amount of household bleach (5%) to add *
1 gal. (4.5 litres)	2 drops (0.18 mL)
2 1/5 gal. (10 litres)	5 drops (0.4 mL)
5 gal. (23 litres)	11 drops (0.9 mL)
10 gal. (45 litres)	22 drops (1.8 mL)
22 gal. (100 litres)	3/4 teaspoon (4 mL)
45 gal. (205 litres)	1 1/2 teaspoons (8 mL)
50 gal. (230 litres)	1 3/4 teaspoons (9 mL)
100 gal. (450 litres)	3 1/2 teaspoons (18 mL)
220 gal. (1000 litres)	8 teaspoons (40 mL)
500 gal. (2200 litres)	6 tablespoons (90 mL)
1000 gal. (4550 litres)	6 1/2 ounces or 12 tablespoons (180 mL)

*Adding household (5%) bleach at these amounts will produce water with about 2 parts per million of chlorine in it (about 0.0002 percent).

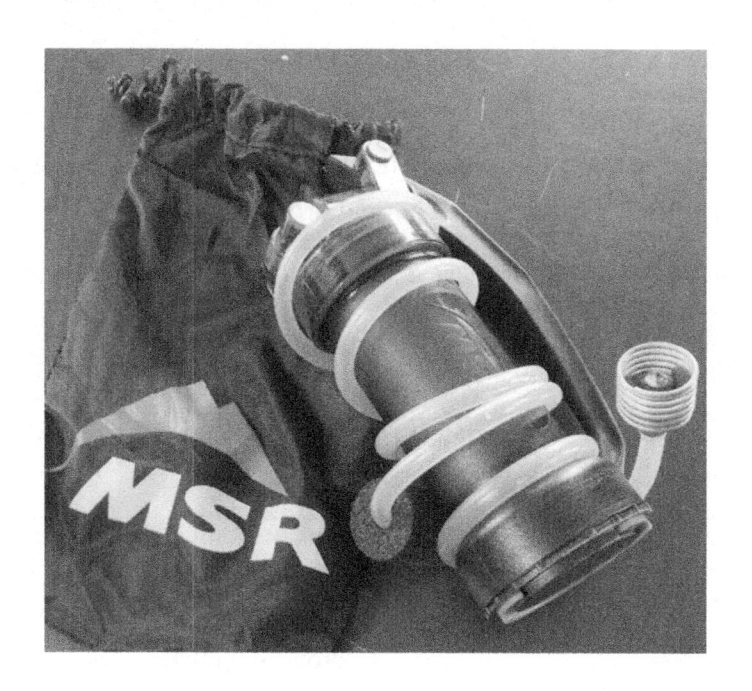

An alternative method when treating larger volumes of water can be a hand-pump ceramic filter, like this MSR model (above), or something like a Big Berkey ceramic gravity-fed filter.

If you have any questions about your drinking water, please contact your local Drinking Water Officer or Health Authority. (Info courtesy of http://www.healthlinkbc.ca)

Minimum Suggestion: A case of bottled water, package of water purification tablets and personal water filter for each member of your family or group and a couple of spares (like a Sawyer mini of LifeStraw). A large pot to boil water in.

FOOD

There is a frightening statistic that I have known about for some time now which puts into perspective how truly fragile our society and its conveniences has become. The following is a breakdown by the American Trucking Association outlining the deterioration of major industries following a truck stoppage:

- First 24 hrs – Gas stations will begin to go dry, hospitals will begin to run out of supplies, mail and package delivery will cease;
- Within one day – Food shortages will begin to develop, fuel availability will become scarce, assembly lines will stop.
- Within 2 to 3 days – food shortages will escalate, essentials (water, powdered milk, canned meat) will disappear, ATMs will run out of cash, gas stations will be dry, garbage will start piling up in urban/suburban areas, container ships and trains will sit idle and transportation will eventually come to a standstill.
- Within a week – Automobile travel will cease due to lack of fuel stopping people from getting to work or to access medical care, hospitals will begin to run out of oxygen and other vital supplies;
- Within two weeks – the nation's clean water supply will begin to run dry;

- Within four weeks – the nation will exhaust its clean water supply and water will be safe for drinking only after boiling. Gastrointestinal illnesses will increase, causing wide-spread sickness.

The above timeline is truly terrifying. To know how much we rely on trucks is bad enough. Shipping (via large ocean-going container and tanker ships) carries ~94% of the WORLD'S economy. Together with trucking, rail and aviation, they make the logistical world go 'round. If trucks can't unload ships (and to a lesser extent, trains and planes, you can't get what you need from anywhere outside your own backyard. You might consider growing some of your own food and preserving it through canning or dehydration. But these considerations are for self-sufficiency planning well beyond the 200hr mark.

In looking at our priorities, we see that we can, if we HAD to, go without food for about 3 weeks. Thus, in preparing for a 200hr disaster, huge stockpiles of food should not be your goal. You should have a stocked pantry of the foods you would normally eat. These should include easily prepared, non-perishable and nutritious foods which will sustain you and your family through the recovery period.

Canned foods, dried goods, staple supplies and high-energy foods are usually best for our perceived disaster. There are some general principles which you should keep in mind when building up your food supply:

- Eat what you store, store what you eat. (If you don't usually eat tuna, don't store it)
- Buy an extra of whatever you usually buy, as put it away in a segmented part of your pantry.
- Rotate your supply as you buy new items so that your disaster supply is always fresh.

- Label additions as you purchase them (Date bought and/or good until).
- Store your foods in containers which will keep them from spoilage or pests.

Look to store high-energy, less-perishable foods that are easy to cook. Don't forget to have a backup manual can opener in your kit!

You should plan your supply according to your group size – just like with water. Figure on 5 meals, per person, per day. The additional 2 meals are considered "snacks", so stock the supply accordingly.

Examples of these types of foods may include the following:

- Flour, sugar, salt, spices, other supplies for baking & cooking
- Canned soups, stews, chili...
- Canned veggies, fruits, fish
- Dehydrated fruits, vegetables and legumes

- Powdered milk, eggs, soup stock/bouillon, steel cut oats, instant mashed potatoes
- Pastas, instant noodles, cup-of-soups
- Beans, legumes (dried or canned)
- Camp foods, MREs (Meals-Ready to-Eat)
- Hard candies, dark chocolate, protein bars
- Coffee, teas, drink crystals, coffee whitener, hot chocolate powder

For the above supplies, consider either a lock seal Tupperware container or something like a Gamma Food Vault. These would ensure that pests cannot get at your food and that they stay dry and avoid spoilage. Don't forget to throw in a desiccant (moisture absorbing) packet and possibly an oxygen absorber if food is being stored for a longer period.

A rock-solid example to examine is the sub-culture of Ultra-lite backpacking. More information on this can be found online.

If you have a solidly stocked pantry and a freezer with a few staples, you can cook the foods thawing in your freezer first and then move on to your pantry supply. This should be able to sustain your caloric needs for the duration of the recovery period.

Whatever you do, don't forget to stock some extra coffee (in this case, Cleared Hot Espresso from Arrowhead Coffee Company (www.arrowhead.coffee), a manual way to grind the beans and a way to brew it. Just because you're going through a disaster doesn't mean you need to suffer unnecessarily!

Minimum Suggestion: Food capable of sustaining your family/group for ~200hrs. (3 meals a day – breakfast, lunch, supper – plus 2 snacks = 25 mcals x per person x 4 =?. Note: this does not include water or drinks) Food should be easily prepared, non-perishable, nutritious, familiar and generally enjoyable.

MEDICAL & FIRST AID

If you haven't already – go take a First Aid & CPR training course. RIGHT NOW!. Okay, now that you're back, let us discuss first aid in the context of a 200hr preparedness plan.

If we are looking at a short-term period of up to 200hrs, our needs from a medical perspective should be relatively modest. Everyone in your group over the age of 13 should have some form of basic first aid training. That, coupled with a comprehensive first aid and medical supply kit should be able to get you through most problems.

If the Event happens to be a storm, flying debris may be a cause of injury. So you should be prepared for cuts, bruises and possibly fractures. A winter storm may be a cause of hypothermia and shock. If you have to cook over an open flame or build a fire for warmth, burns may be a hazard. A comprehensive and well-stocked first aid kit should address these concerns. The supplies, along with your training. Remember to focus on the task at hand if something happens, remember your training and KEEP PANIC IN CHECK!

In a large-scale disaster scenario, the most commonly encountered injuries tend to be:

- Cuts, punctures (bleeding control)
- Joint injuries (hands, ankles, knees)
- Burns
- Infections
- Environmental injuries (Dehydration, hypothermia, heat exhaustion)
- Broken bones

First aid kits are available from most drug stores, big-box stores, camping and industrial stores as well as online retailers (such as CTOMS Inc. and Ragnarok Tactical). These are usually generic and may not meet your needs if you have specific hazards which you feel you may be at higher risk for. Consider your group, the specific needs of all you may be responsible and then factor in the possible hazards you may face in the 200hrs you would be on your own. Personally, I recommend a small generic kit that you then augment and tailor to cover your specific circumstances (See example below).

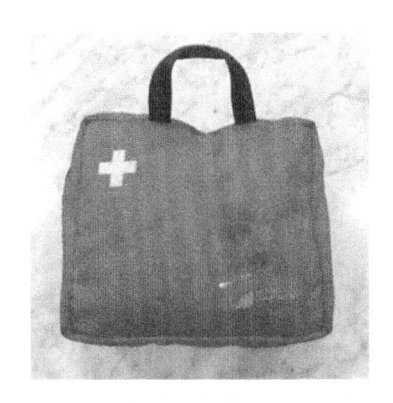

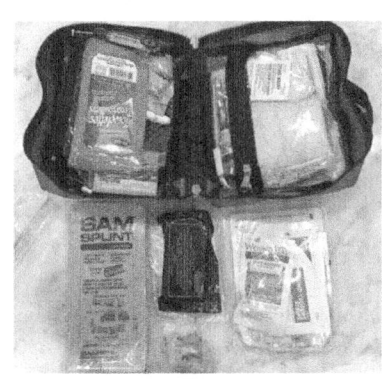

NOTE: Always remember your ABCs:
- Airway
- Bleeding
- Circulation

A general first aid kit may contain the following:

- Duct tape
- Latex or Nitrile gloves (Some people have allergies to latex. Nitrile are a better option)
- Various bandages (I prefer cloth, they are more flexible and less prone to allergic reactions)
- CPR face shield
- Sterile gauze pads (also consider maxi-pads as a field bandage)
- Non-adherent gauze rolls and dressings
- Butterfly strips (for wound closure)
- Pre-formed finger gauze wraps and bandages (Very good to have)Instant Cold packs / freezer packs for burns and other injuries
- First aid tape
- Kling wrap – self-adhering roller bandage
- Moleskin (for blisters)
- Safety pins (several, in various sizes)
- Irrigation syringe (to clean wounds)
- Triple Antibiotic ointment
- Topical antiseptic towelettes / alcohol wipes
- Iodine (10% tincture) (Caution: Iodine can cause allergic reactions)
- Rubbing alcohol
- Hydrogen Peroxide (Best option for disinfectant)
- Elastic "tensor-style" bandages (different sizes)
- Soap and hand sanitizer (Non-scented)
- Féminine hygiene products (tampons/pads, etc)
- Tweezers
- Small scissors or EMT shears – (curved & straight)

- Lighter or pack of matches
- A few pins/needles
- Hydrocortisone cream
- Insect repellant
- Sunscreen, Noxzema & Aloe gel (100% aloe is best)
- Scalpel or a few razor blades
- Small notebook and pencil, permanent marker
- Small flashlight or headlamp dedicated to first aid kit
- Tourniquet (high quality)   ***GET TRAINING AND KNOW HOW TO USE IT***
- Bandana
- Triangular bandages
- Packets of QuikClot (Hemostatic blood clotting agent)
- Instant Cold & Heat packs
- Thermometer (non-battery operated at a minimum)
- SAM Splint or functional alternative
- Face masks (N-95)
- Suture Kit (optional, if trained)
- Emergency Dental kit
- Baby wipes (flushable, bio-degradable)
- Diaper rash cream (Desitin, Zincofax, Wellskin, - Zinc-oxide cream)
- Anti-friction cream (Balm blaster, hydropel, etc)
- Silicon anti-blister band-aids for your feet (excellent to have)
- Tourniquet (learn to use it and get a quality one! Don't skimp when lives may be on the line!)
- Comprehensive first aid manual and reference book
- Container to hold it all (labeled and in a conspicuous area)

- **TRAINING, TRAINING, TRAINING!** (Check local community colleges, outdoor groups, outdoor stores, St. John Ambulance, Red Cross, etc. Also, Stop The BleedTM training and any emergency medical training you can get.)

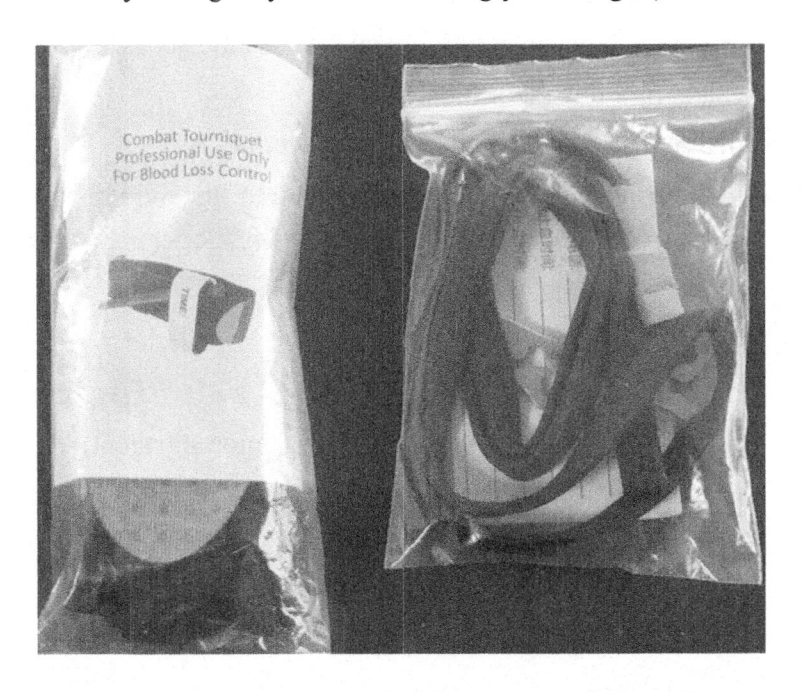

Tourniquets (like those pictured above) should be a part of your first aid kits in your home, vehicle and workplace. Get trained, get equipped with quality gear and be prepared to render aid. The life you save may be your own or that of someone you love. Stopping bleeding is a paramount skill towards saving lives when emergency medical assistance may not be available due to a disaster event.

Breaking down your first aid kit into easily accessible layers may be beneficial to remain organized and to have the needed resources to deal with the situation at hand.

Level 1: Every day cuts, scrapes pain. The most commonly used items.

Level 2: Medium sized and less-often used items to the second layer.

Level 3: Emergency medical care for serious wounds, shock, etc.

Also, ensure that you have additional medications for those in your group. You should have supplies for any critical medical needs you may experience.

These may include, but are not limited to:

- Ventolin (salbutamol) inhalers
- Insulin & syringes
- Epi – Pens
- Pain medications – Tylenol (Acetaminophen), Advil (Ibuprofen), Aleve (Naproxin)
- Nitroglycerin (ask your doctor)
- Antibiotic ointments (such as Polysporin)
- Birth control - pills, condoms, etc.
- anti-histamines (Claritin, Reactine, Benadryl, Aerius) Go with a non-drowsy formula
- anti-diarrhea meds (Immodium)
- anti-nausea pills or suppositories (Gravol – to prevent vomiting)
- Decongestants
- Antacids (Tums)
- Laxative tablets (Senokot)
- Cough drops
- Antibiotics (if available – ask your physician)
- Oral rehydration solution (Pedialite) to replace Electrolytes lost from dehydration by exertion, vomiting or diarrhea.
- Full-spectrum multi-vitamins for all.

- RadBlock (Potassium Iodide Tablets) for those living near nuclear facilities or in the path of projected fallout zones. RadBlock blocks the absorption of radioactive iodine. Most jurisdictions' Public Health Units which may be affected but this often provide residents this medication free of charge. (See image below). One of the developments which have come from the Russian invasion of Ukraine has been the insecurity of nuclear installations across Ukraine and how damage to their structures could affect the country and Europe as well. Remember Chernobyl? If you live anywhere near a nuclear facility or in the path of fallout from one, consider reaching out to your local public health unit (or to the facility management arm) and request tabs. In Toronto, Ki tabs can be ordered at https://preparetobesafe.ca/order .

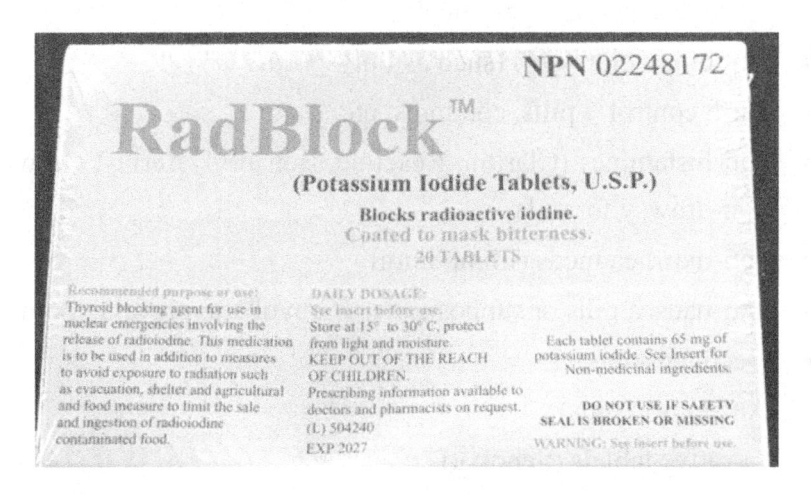

To go into some more specifics with respect to the list above:

- **Aspirin** (acetylsalicylic acid / ASA): not recommended for pain. May cause internal bleeding. Best to give to heart attack victims at on-set.
- **Tylenol** (acetaminophen): Best as pain relief and to reduce fever.

- **Advil** (ibuprofen): Also for pain relief and as an anti-inflammatory.
- **Aleve** (naproxen): Also for pain relief and anti-inflammatory.
- **Anti-biotic cream**: broad-spectrum recommended (Baciguent, Fucidin)
- **Anti-histamine:** for prevention of hives, rashes and allergic reactions. Claratin, Aerius are best. Benadryl is good but causes drowsiness.
- **Decongestant (psudoephedrine):** for treatment of upper-respiratory infections. Flu/fever/cold/sore throat/runny nose/etc. Causes drowsiness but very effective. Advil Cold & Sinus or comparable alternative. Not recommended for <12 yrs old.
- **Anti-biotics:** MAY CAUSE ADVERSE EFFECTS OR HARMFUL ALLERGIC REACTIONS. CONSULT A PHYSICIAN ON USE OF SYSTEMIC ANTI-BIOTICS.
- **Stereroid Cream** (hydro-cortisone 1-2.5% active): For skin inflammation, allergic reactions, Sunburns (not burns). Not to be applied to open sores or wounds. Ointments for dry skin and lesions, Creams for where skin folds or rubs together.
- **Anti-Diarrhea**: (Immodium Advanced) Also contains additives to prevent cramping.

So, to recap, go get some training, put together some ready supplies and get to a level of proficiency where you will feel comfortable dealing with first-aid situations.

DISCLAIMER *Prior to acquiring or taking any suggested medications discuss it with a certified medical professional to ensure it is right for you and your personal situation. These are suggestions only and are generic in their applicability and are not meant to replace qualified medical advice.*

Minimum Suggestion: Take a First-Aid course. Then, either build or purchase an adequate first aid kit for your needs and maintain its contents for freshness. Consult with a qualified medical practitioner for medicines and any other components prior to use.

HEALTH, SANITATION & HYGIENE

No, you are not re-reading the previous chapter. One very often-overlooked facet of a disaster scenario is keeping ourselves clean, maintaining a sanitary environment around us and dealing with human waste. Ultimately, the end goal of this book and disaster planning in general, is to sustain health (and life) through an austere ordeal.

In many Third World places, much of the disease endured by people there are directly related to poor sanitation. Polluted water, infection of minor injuries and parasitic infections and ineffective sewage management are all killers without ready access to effective treatment.

Keeping cleaning supplies and using them to maintain a clean environment can stave off disease, as well as vermin.

Washing your hands and maintaining a sanitary living environment can save you the hassle and suffering of fecal and food-borne illnesses. This is also highly effective in preventing the spread of bacteria and viruses to others and them to you. Simple bar soap, hand sanitizer, bleach solutions, rubbing alcohol, hydrogen peroxide and the like are all effective means of controlling the spread of infection and disease. Despite the hype, "good 'lo fashioned" hand washing (soap, lather, scrub for 20+ seconds and rinse) is the most effective and simple means of preventing this. Steer away from fancy scented soaps and stick with simple and effective soaps that can keep for a long time and still get the job done.

If you or someone in your group does become ill, treat them as best you can with the first-aid supplies you have respecting their symptoms. Follow whatever first aid training you have (did you go yet?) and refer to medical professionals and reference material if available. I highly recommend acquiring a medical reference book and keeping it to assist in diagnosing symptoms in a disaster scenario until proper health arrives.

(Note: This should by no means take the place of professional medical assistance and opinion and should only be used when no professional medical assistance is forthcoming.) Maintain hydration and promote rest. These two are of great importance when fighting most illnesses.

Tired? REST! Fatigue increases the chances of errors and poor judgment. If you are tired, sleep. Caffeine is not sleep.

If the water shuts off the dirty truth is that your toilets will stop working. Though most toilets are gravity-fed and can be flushed by pouring a bucket of water directly into the bowl, the reservoir will not re-fill. Another issue you might face is the sewers may back up without a working power grid.

Note: You may have the option of installing a "back-flow valve" to prevent back flow of sewage into your home. Some municipalities have offered a subsidy for people looking to upgrade their plumbing with a back-flow valve and will reimburse the home owner after the work has been completed. If this is not an option, consider opening up the drain and stuffing it with a towel to prevent back flow on a short-term basis. ***Speak to a certified plumber for expert advice on this.***

A stock of tough garbage bags can do double duty (pardon the pun) for both back-up sanitation as well as provide plastic sheeting for everything from rain catchments, sealing windows and even makeshift sleeping bags.

Prepare to take care of your business on your own. If you are on a septic/gravity fed system of sewage management and have a ready supply of water (either from a lake, river or other reliable source of water) you may consider using grey water to deal with your solid human waste. Count yourself as fortunate for this particular situation.

If not, there are various ways of dealing with this particularly unsavory chore. Consider the following for your situation:

- **Chemical Waste Treatments** – to be used in conjunction with plastic pails and heavy-duty (pun intended) garbage bags. These come in home-made and commercially available versions. By lining the pail with a garbage bag and pouring a bit of bleach and liquid detergent you can do your business and tie it up later for disposal. Commercial products (such as the "Double Doodie" toilet liner bag) contain a chemical waste liquefier and disinfectant in the bag and are easier to manage, though may cost more.
- **Natural Waste Treatments** – Same basic pail & bag set-up as above, but instead use kitty litter, crushed/damp leaves, wet grass or coarse saw dust as a filler to cover up each "deposit".
- **Latrine dug-out** – If you have the space outdoors, you may consider digging a latrine. You would be looking at a trench about 1-2 feet deep and about 1 foot wide. The length or number of latrines is dependent on the number of people you have to deal with, though 1 should suffice for ~100 hrs. If it's just you and one other, you can make-do with a 2×2 foot cat hole and manage it accordingly.

Pandemic Considerations: In the event of an imminent pandemic threat, there are a few additional things that you may want to consider: Wear suitable footwear during an emergency. Solid tread to prevent slips and to be resistant to punctures.

- Create distance from other people to avoid contamination or infection.
- Wash your hands regularly.
- Wear a mask to protect yourself and others.

- Wear gloves to protect your hands from cuts and pathogens.
- Eye mask or glasses to protect against spray/particulate.
- Consider an apron or rain suit to protect against contaminated fluids.
- Consider wearing an N-95 mask if traveling through crowds or in close proximity with others.
- Depending on the situation, something like a 3M respirator with appropriate filter. (This may be overboard, but I'm presenting it anyways.)

Toilet paper (aka White Gold). You can never have enough. You also take it for granted until you run out.

Speaking of health, here is a thought to ponder about your health and welfare during a disaster scenario. One thing that can make a massive difference in one's ability to negotiate a difficult time is their level of health and fitness prior to the event occurring. This is important. Health and wellness, or fitness if you will, is a measure of the body's resilience against illness and fatigue. These two challenges are omnipresent during a disaster and the better you are able to cope with prolonged periods of work, fatigue, injuries, stress, lack of sleep, lack of food, and sickness. The problem with this is that achieving a healthy level of fitness is a lifestyle choice that occurs before an event. You can't just smash a Monster Energy Drink or a Red Bull and suddenly you're Captain America. No, that'll cause you more harm than good. Leading a healthy, active lifestyle before you're put to the test is resilience and longevity insurance. Get on it now and enjoy the benefits for years to come. And if the time comes when you're in the clinch, you'll be far better off than those who chose the Netflix and donuts. Just my 2 cents.

<u>Minimum Suggestion</u>: A plastic pail, package of heavy-duty garbage bags and bottle of chlorine bleach. A few spare bars of soap and a bottle of hand sanitizer. N-95 masks and goggles. And a healthy lifestyle, body and mind going into the event.

COMMUNICATIONS

Communication during a time of emergency or disaster can be both a convenience and a necessity. Knowing what is going on – through news and weather reports, public safety announcements and through friends or family – can be either heart warming or life saving. Knowing about an incoming hurricane or tsunami may be the difference between getting out in time or being wiped out. Communications allow you to call for help when needed. Having various forms of communication with your friends, family and the world outside your four walls may allow you to be heard or to hear others when regular telephone, cable and cellular networks are down.

Having a back-up for this purpose is a smart preparation to make and need not be expensive. In wanting to be able to reach others there are many options. There are several methods of two-way radio communication available to the regular consumer. These include:

- Satellite phones
- Dual-band VHF/UHF (Very-high frequency/Ultra-high frequency) radios;
- FRS/GMRS radios;
- Citizen Band (CB) radios; are all viable options for the everyday.

- More complex and robust Amateur Radios (in the HF or High Frequency Band) are available but their use is usually restricted to licensed individuals. For more information on Amateur Radio, visit the Industry Canada website (www.ic.gc.ca).
- For local use, simplicity and cost, the FRS/GMRS family of radios should be sufficient.
- Though technically illegal under regular circumstances, you should be able to use Marine-band VHF radios for two-way communications in a disaster situation, but if your life depends on it, you may decide to use the Marine emergency band to get a distress call out.

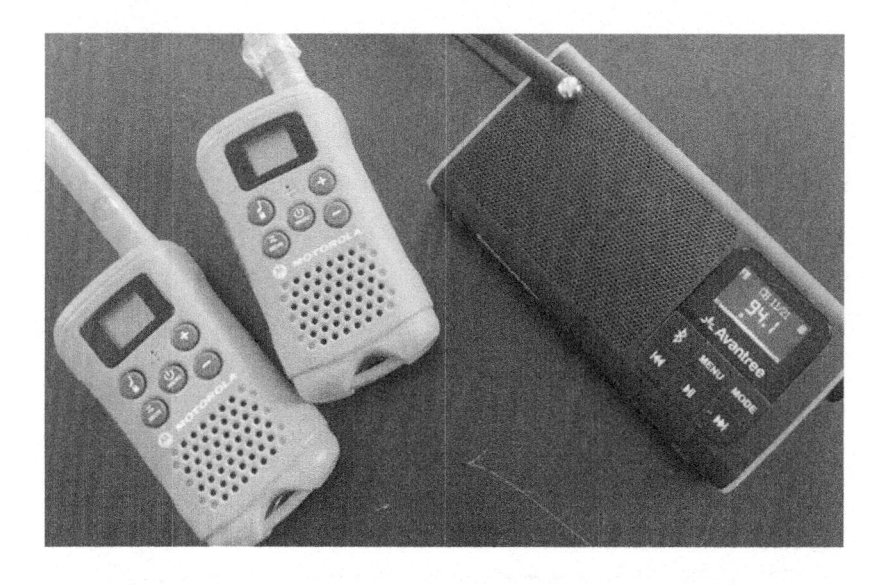

Simple radio setup. The example (above) of a battery-powered radio (right) to get local news and disaster information and a pair of FRS walkie-talkies (left) to both scan the airwaves and communicate with.

Additionally, if you want to stay informed when the lights go out, consider buying a battery, hand-crank or solar-powered radio, weather radio, short-wave radio and possibly a radio frequency scanner will allow you to listen to local radio broadcasts and stay informed as to the goings on of the emerging situation.

***TIP*: *During an emergency, cellular & telephone lines and voice communications can become jammed with a high volume of calls, making it almost impossible to get through to someone. Text/SMS messages often make it through when voice calls fail.*

Again, there are pros and cons to each. Some weather radios have a function which will sound an alarm in the event of an incoming severe weather system. Short Wave radio receivers will pick up signals from all around the globe giving you a valuable source of information should the local radio stations go off the air due to the emergency. Radio scanners allow you to listen in to a very wide spectrum of frequencies. These can also include local police, fire and emergency services as well as radio stations and short wave.

The importance of accurate and timely information cannot be overstated, especially if timeliness means the difference between evacuating in the face of a raging wildfire of being cut off from escape from finding out too late.

Another thing you may consider having with you is a camera. You can use it to record the condition you left your home in, or damage to it (for insurance claims later on) or to record the ordeal for future use.

As previously stated, you should have some means of contact with the outside world in the case of an emergency where regular (Internet, telephone and cellular) networks are inoperative. Make sure you assess your level of need, your budget for communications and then buy the best system for you. Do the research, go to the stores and try the various systems out. Ask questions and read reviews. Invest wisely.

***TIP** – *Some areas (Provinces, States or cities) offer its residents to sign up for text and email alerts regarding disaster and emergency* *alerts for their areas. Things like tornado and winter storm warnings will be sent out via SMS text message and/or e-mail at the first sign of trouble.*

Minimum Suggestion: Have a battery/solar/hand-crank radio to listen to local weather and news broadcasts when the power grid is down. Look for one that can charge your cell phone through an auxiliary USB jack.

LIGHT, ELECTRICITY & BACK-UPS

When the power goes out, that usually means so do the lights. Having a reliable source of light in times of darkness is essential. Not only does it make things safer (everything from tasks to merely walking around your house) but also creates a level of psychological comfort to those around it. Again, your methods of light production need not be expensive, only reliable.

Simple, effective, inexpensive solar and hand-crank LED lantern (above). Perfect for your balcony and emergency power outages.

*****TIP**: Natural gas does not require electricity to operate. Even in the case of an emergency, as long as the gas lines are intact, there could be enough in the lines for days or even weeks to accommodate cooking and heating. There are even natural gas-powered stand-by generators which run on natural gas. The downside is that furnaces and water pumps require electricity to work. Try to use your gas oven or gas fireplace for heating and cooking. Just make sure your smoke and carbon monoxide detectors are working properly.*****

In-line, natural gas emergency backup generators (like the one pictured above) is available through places like Home Depot. They are robust, reliable and will power your entire home with natural gas which keeps flowing in the event of a power outage.

Candles, flashlights, headlamps, lanterns, hand-crank & solar lights, fire, chemical lights & oil lamps are all viable reserve options for providing emergency lighting for a short-term basis. Ensure that you have appropriate units, fuel, batteries, matches/lighters to be able to sustain use for the needed period of the disaster. Special care needs to be given for handling of flammable materials and ensuring that fuel-powered light sources are not left unattended as this can cause fires and lead to injury and/or death.

Your local Costco (above-left) and Canadian Tire (above-right) have a plethora of options when it comes to inexpensive and reliable backup lighting options.

Tip: *Keep your vehicle(s) as topped-off with fuel as possible and store extra fuel in cans at home. Fuel will be at a premium during an* *emergency and you don't want to be running out. Also stock a seasonally-themed vehicle emergency kit in your trunk.****

Your lighting backup can be as simple as a box of candles and a couple of flashlights with spare batteries. These should be able to last you through the 200-hour period without much of a problem (with disciplined use). More back-ups should mean more options to be comfortable through the ordeal. Consider stocking several rechargeable batteries in the most common sizes you regularly use and consider a solar-powered recharging unit. There are also lights which have built-in solar panels and internal rechargeable batteries which will work indefinitely. They can be inexpensive and offer many varieties for your various needs so stock up and have plentiful, redundant lighting for all your needs.

As many homes are dependent upon electricity for their cooking, heating and feeding needs, consideration should be paid towards redundancy in those areas. As yourself the following questions to address these needs:

- How will I cook my food / boil water?
- How will I keep warm?
- What will I do for light after the sun goes down?
- Can I power any electrical equipment (tools, machines, radios, etc) when the power goes out?
- What is my back-up for this eventuality?
- Is my system complex? Does it require maintenance or expertise to operate?
- How sustainable is my system?
- What are the associated costs for my back-up options?

After you have been able to thoroughly answer the above, choose the option(s) best suited to your situation and budget and begin implementation.

Some households may have the option (or already have in place) back-ups of various varieties. These may include stand-by generators, solar panel arrays, geo-thermal systems, micro-hydro and/or windmill technologies. Such back-ups can be scald from the small and simple (pocket solar panel for phone/laptop) to the expensive and involved (generator backups, multiple-panel solar arrays, windmill generators). Do take a look at your situation and ascertain the level of power backup you need. Small solar panels may be able to meet basic needs if hooked up to low-wattage LED light strings and inverters to charge handheld devices. These need not be expensive and are available at places like Canadian Tire, Costco, on Amazon and the like. There are even some that clip on to your backpack for hiking that will do the trick.

Examples of portable solar panels (above) which are cheap and effective at providing backup power for small devices, phones and LED lights.

You can pair these portable battery power banks (above) with the solar panels to have power for your devices, as long as you have adapters for them.

Make an effort to standardize your electronic devices so that they all share as few different types of batteries. Stock that particular type so that you will be able to maintain operability across your devices. AA batteries are readily available, comparatively inexpensive and come in rechargeable varieties that can power just about anything you'd have around your home.

Stock up on some reliable batteries for your devices and rotate them to maintain freshness. The Duracells

(above) work well and are relatively inexpensive when purchased at Big Box stores.

Minimum Suggestion: Have a means to keep essential electrical units running and possibly to run your fridge, water and furnace motors and any other essential pieces of equipment. Either a generator or many independent power pack options & batteries.

SECURITY

There are many works dedicated to the topic of home and personal security. I myself could go on for days about recommendations, principles, tips, etc, but that is for the next book. In the context of disaster and emergency preparedness, Security is specifically focused on threats from aggressive human actors and, to a far lesser extent, hostile wildlife.

To the extent which wildlife can be a threat in an urban or suburban environment, your home should provide sufficient protection from hungry or aggressive animals seeking food or shelter. If you life in an area where encounters with potentially dangerous animal life is likely, you may consider procuring a firearm or similar weapon (such as a crossbow or bow), getting training and storing it safely in case you need to defend your home or property from harm. This scenario could present itself at any time and need not be limited to a disaster scenario. I would suggest this would be limited to animals like bears, coyotes, wolves,, dogs, large wild cats, raccoons, opossums, and rabid varieties of the aforementioned.

To a greater extent during a disaster situation, the threat of desperate human predators increases proportionally as the Rule of Law decreases. Where those who provide the thin veneer of societal security head home to protect their families, those who would prey upon others and cause harm will feel emboldened to do what they will. Everything from harm for the sake of harm to theft of resources to simple desperation. Hungry and scared people will do things they wouldn't usually do under "regular" circumstances. Seeing their children starving or sick without medication can change that.

With these things in mind, your preparations should be shielded from general view and not be common knowledge to those around you whom you do not trust. In the event of a disaster, you, being well-prepared and stocked can become an instant target to a desperate person who did not think to prepare beforehand. This is called Operational Security (or OPSEC for short) and is the control of information about what you have, how much of it, where it is stored, what your emergency plans are and how you would plan to weather a storm. This information can be used against you as those who are without start to angrily demand you share your supplies with them at gun point. If you seem to be just as down and out as the rest of your community (just getting by) then you have a better chance of not becoming a target.

OPSEC can be maintained by keeping information about your preparations confidential and "need-to-know", restricted only to those in your immediate circle of trust and the out-of-town safety you have established.

This requires discipline. If you have a backup generator and all the lights are out in your neighborhood, consider not running it in the night and lighting up your house. Do what the rest of the population around you is doing. Do practice light and sound discipline. Don't draw unwanted attention towards yourself and your level of preparedness. Another giveaway is garbage discipline. If the garbage you are throwing out tells a different story from what you are telling your neighbors, someone will get suspicious and may target you. This is also sometimes referred to as the "grey man" principle. A "grey man" is someone who blends into their environment, drawls little to no attention, is difficult to recall and gives off no memorable stimuli to remember. The kind of person who is referred to as "average". Keeping a low profile and not attracting attention to yourself is sometimes called the "Grey Man Principle", which seeks mitigate readily observable stimuli when traversing the urban landscape. This means not sticking out. Not appearing to show signs of wealth, health, features that stand out – just a bland, forgettable figure at one with the background which no one pays attention to. Think about someone wearing a safety vest and carrying a clipboard at a construction site. They're basically invisible. That's what you want, for no one to give you a second (or hopefully a first) glance and take notice.

If you are the kind of person who is not of "average" disposition, you can take steps to fix this and change your outward appearance and interactions through a revision of your behavior. When it comes to clothes, think bland. Take labels and tags of clothing. Subdue features and stitching with a marker or dirt. Don't wear jewelry, expensive watches or carry "tactical" gear as these indicators may be taken as wealth by someone who may then look at you as a target. Looking "Grey Man" obfuscates these indicators and allows you to blend into the background of someone looking for people who stand out, looking for a target.

The same goes for your home. Expensive cars in the driveway, fancy landscaping, and lots of lights on while the rest of the neighborhood is in darkness draws the wrong kind of attention after a few days. Consider letting some stuff go and disciplining yourself to a "Grey Man" goal.

Maintain sound physical security of your home. In regular life (pre-disaster):

- Invest in quality locks (the higher security the better) and reinforced door hardware installed by a qualified locksmith or security professional;
- set-up adequate lighting around your house giving you good visibility at night while removing shadows and obstacles from a potential threat from hiding;
- Invest in security cameras with night-vision capabilities (these may deter thieves until the power goes out);
- Set-up early warning devices on your property (such as solar-powered motion lights giving you a complete perimeter coverage of your home. If you have a fence around your home, those self-contained solar-powered motion lights can be placed on poles around your property giving illumination over the target area but also directs your attention to a possible intrusion site.
- Get a dog. Few things are as vigilant, accurate and detrimental to a potential trespasser as a dog. Even a small yappy dog will know when someone has stepped over the line and intruded onto your property, and they'll let you and the intruder know you know. With the element of surprise gone and the chance of prepared defense, the odds of a "soft target" becoming a very "hard target" increase greatly. Most criminal elements are looking for easy scores. A prepared, well-fortified and warned house is a scary place to attempt to break into when you don't know what's on the other side of the door.
- Consider personal defense training and possibly a firearm to protect yourself, family and home in case of home invasion or break-in during a disaster. ***THIS IS A PERSONAL DECISION AND IS YOUR RESPONSIBILITY TO KNOW THE RISKS, LEGALITIES AND RESPONSIBILITIES

ASSOCIATED WITH FIREARMS OWNERSHIP AND USE OF FORCE. CONSULT COMPETENT INDEPENDENT LEGAL ADVICE***

- If possible (and safe to do so) arrange a "buddy system" with a close neighbor to mutually protect each others homes and families in the event of a security incident. If you're both firearms owners, establish common procedures, Rules of Engagement and communications protocols.

- With respect to types of firearms for "home defense", I won't even wade into those waters in this forum. You need training, storage, licensing and a few dollars to make a purchase. Then you need to practice and practice some more. If you are unfortunate enough to find yourself in an altercation involving a firearm and causing harm with it, you must be fully aware of the legal ramifications of using such force. This may be slightly diminished if you are buying a firearm for protection from wildlife (research the legalities of discharging a firearm in your district, if allowable at all), but do understand that the use of the same firearm against a human is altogether different. Get competent legal advice and take the approved safety courses.

- Learn about physical security and non-destructive entry (such as lock picking). There may be times when, in order to save a life or prevent harm, a resource is available, but access to it is prevented by a lock. (Such as a life-saving medication for a child). In such an instance, I would consider the non-destructive access to such a resource acceptable. Don't steal, pay for it, lock up behind you, leave a note. But you never know when, either at home or abroad, a lock is something that stands between death and life. ***I am not advocating breaking and entering nor am I advocating theft in any way, however, having the skills to access something to help someone or yourself and using those skills in exigent circumstances may trump the alternative. Something to think about. These skills and associated knowledge can also be used to close the gaps in your own security picture when at home or when traveling.

The above points are guidelines only and demand much greater attention and consideration. You must be aware of your local laws, requirements and responsibilities to ensure the safety of yourself and others.

PREPARATIONS FOR SMALL SPACES: CONDOS & APARTMENTS

For those living in condos and apartments within the urban and suburban environment, the challenge of space being at a premium is one of the foremost challenges to successfully prepare for a disaster scenario – even for a week.

In this section, I will re-hash the principles of this book thus far and reframe them for a condo or apartment situation. For the sake of simplicity, I will use the word "condo" to reference all living units that would fall under the category of condominium unit, loft, apartment, townhouse, cooperative unit, etc – anything where your living space is a block within a larger structure and not having it's own independent utilities, yard, footprint and the like.

Effective disaster prepping in a small space is similar to living in a small space. You have to establish priorities, carefully plan and be disciplined in the execution of that plan. It can be done, but needs to be done smartly because your space is at a premium.

First off, get organized. Tidy your apartment. Clean out the stuff you don't need. Take stock of what you have, what you don't have and what you need.

Every living space, no matter the size, should have a basic set of tools in it to affect basic repairs and generally make things happen. Without basic tools, you'll be at a huge disadvantage. If you are a parent thinking about what to get your kid for a present as they leave for post-secondary schooling or are moving away for a job and getting their own place, consider a toolbox filled with basic, quality tools, some common nails, screws, plugs, some duct tape, crazy glue, WD40 and the like. If they take care of it, it'll last a lifetime.

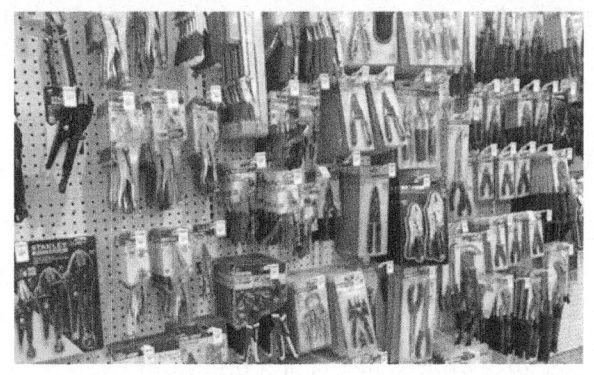

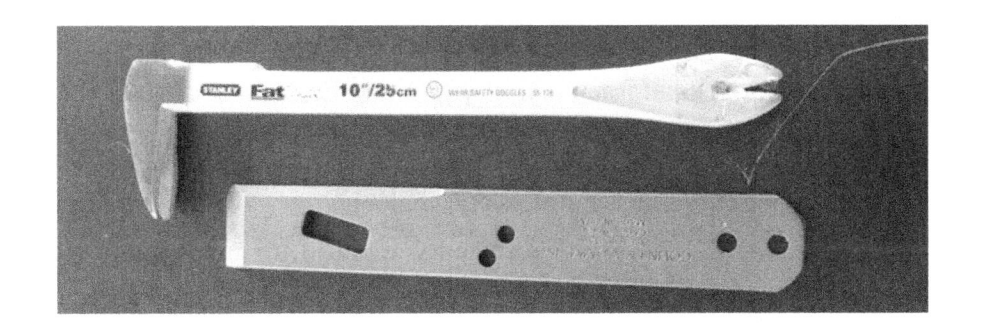

Image 1 of 3 (top) shows a very basic tool layout including a multi-head screwdriver, hammer, pliers, wrench, hex-key set, crazy glue, measuring tape and single Phillips head screwdriver. The Middle image shows a selection of tools available at your local Canadian Tire which, if building just a simple toolkit, need not be expensive. The third image (above) shows a crow bar (top) and flat pry bar with chisel edge and rectangular slot to turn off gas lines with.

Create a list of priorities – what events are you planning for snd what resources you have available. Consider the factors which affect you (building location, neighbourhood (is it a rough one or generally safer), population density, proximity to water sources (like a lake, river or pond) and wooded areas, local resources (like pharmacies, gas stations, Fire/EMS/Police stations and military establishments, veterinary and walk-in clinics, grocery stores and small shops of note, hospitals, etc.) and known hazards & threats) and use those as considerations in making your plans. Note the floor you're on, and if you can be reached by fire trucks. Note how many flights of stairs you have to get from your unit to ground-level, and how long it takes you to get there. Also consider how long and how difficult it is to get from the ground floor to your unit. If your elevator is inoperable and you live on the 27th floor, getting supplies and carrying them back up with you suddenly becomes a lot more of a logistical issue than if you're on the 2nd floor.

In the event of a power failure, consider a solar power array with deep-cycle battery and inverter set up on your balcony or against the window with the most sun exposure. These units come in all manner of size. Some fit in your pocket and expand to collect the sun's rays. Others are a couple of square meters in size, assembled in pieces and require a large stand to hold them. There are some small inverter generators which are much more quiet than traditional backup generators, however, they do still make noise, draw attention, require ventilation (on your balcony) and a small stockpile of extra fuel.

There are many generator options – check which one may work for you.

Depending on your needs and storage options, you can make an informed decision. Your backup lighting can be LEDs which use very little wattage but do the job in a pinch. You can also keep small devices (phone, radio, computer) charged and in-service to stay in touch, get information about the situation and even call for help. You can also buy solar-powered products to set on your window sills and charge so that they are always ready in the event of a black-out. Think about the solar-powered LED garden lights you can find at IKEA and other such places. The path lights there can be used in your balcony garden and then brought inside to be used for light should you need it. You can even store and set up your solar array on the balcony and run the wires in through a window if needed. The equipment takes up little space and the solar panel folds flat and is quickly deployable.

Information is important during an event, so don't forget both a radio that gets AM/FM to hear the news and possibly a HAM, CB or VHF radio (maybe a scanner if you're so inclined) to be able to communicate beyond the usual cellular phone and internet channels. Even a pair of FRS walkie-talkies, when set on monitor, can pick up chatter and give you some information about what's going on around you.

Instal smoke and carbon monoxide detectors, as well as fire extinguishers and maybe fire blankets. If you're low enough to the ground, you may invest in a fire ladder which can be deployed from your balcony and aid in your evacuation during a fire.

If allowed, beef-up your unit security by installing cameras, motion sensors and alarms to protect and give advanced warning of an intruder. See if these can be tied into a back-up power source or be solar-powered. You can also look into installing secondary locking systems and upgrading your locks on the windows, sliding doors and main door if possible.

If you have a balcony, use it! It is extra space that you can cook on, capture water with and put a backup toilet on. You can buy a rain barrel and keep it on your balcony. Even a piece of plastic sheeting or an awning leading to a makeshift eaves trough can direct water into your rain barrel passively. This setup allows you to have a large (55 gal) supply of water at any time (you just need to purify it) and doubles as a passive irrigation source if you decide to use the balcony to grow food in containers.

A rain barrel (pictured above) can direct rainwater and store it for later use to irrigate container gardens, flush toilets and provide drinking water (if properly treated).

In addition to the rain barrel idea, having a Water BOB (or similar bathtub-sized food-grade water bladder) allows you to quickly store a vast quantity of potable water (before the rest of the building drains the system) and keep it from contamination. A standard bathtub holds ~110 gal (about 416 Litres) and if you manage to capture that much clean, potable water then you're well ahead of the curve. This amount, figuring that the average person needs approximately 2 gallons per day, would allow up to 7 (!) people drinking water for a week! So, if it's just a couple of you and a dog, you're sitting pretty for that time. This, along with a couple of water filters or something larger, like a Big Berkey gravity filter, would have you sorted out for potable water. If your unit happens to have it's own hot water tank you can bleed it for additional water.

In addition to your usual linens, incorporate a duvet for the wintertime. Something big, fluffy and down-filled. Or a sleeping bag. In case the heat goes out in winter, you'll be able to stay warm.

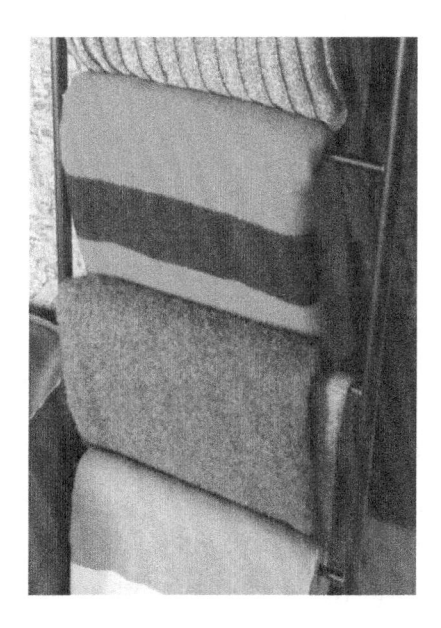

You can store your blankets (pictured right) in a space-saving manner while maintaining a sense of style, all the while being incredibly practical.

For sanitation, ensure that you always have an extra stock of toilet paper (what you would normally go through in 2 weeks as a reserve) on top of your normal supply as well as wet wipes and a back-up toilet (like the pail, liners and kitty litter etc. on the balcony). Your toilet will not function without the incoming water supply, so if you have a rain barrel full of water and a Water BOB in your tub, you can use the rain barrel for the toilet and the clean tub water for cooking and drinking.

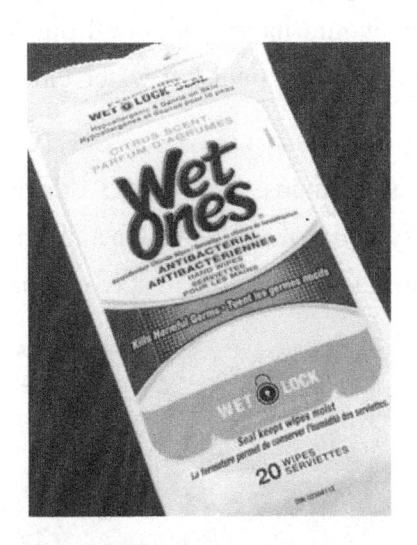

Anti-bacterial wipes (like the Wet Ones, pictured here) are easy sanitary solutions on the go.

Stock your pantry with high-calorie and high-nutrient foods that are non or less-perishable (dry or canned) and rotate regularly. Ideally they should be easy to prepare and can, if needed, be eaten cold. Your balcony can also double as a freezer in winter if the temperature is sufficiently cold, instead of letting the food in your fridge spoil due to power failure. Just make sure pesky raccoons, pigeons and rats can't get at it – get a bin to hold the food.

Ensure that those with special needs, such as children, elderly, infirm, disabled, and pets, are considered and planned for. If medications are needed, stock extra to get you through a week or more. With a pet, have an extra week worth of food stored away. The last thing you need is splitting your food with your dog and running out too soon.

You can use your balcony (or properly positioned windows) to observe the city below and see what's happening. If you live in a complex, you might be able to observe others in the area and gather information about how things are going.

With the above point, do what you can to deter others from gathering information about your situation. Draw the blinds, don't use lights when you don't have to. Practice OPSEC at all times and try not to cook using strong smelling foods. Get a pair of binoculars or spotting scope to observe from a distance. If you want next-level capabilities, you can look at night vision and thermal vision optics with IR (infra-red) and laser add-ons. These pair nicely with home defense weapons in the dark, but I digress – that's a different book altogether.

If you have access to a storage locker associated with your condo unit, you can use it to store some of your less-important materials. Ensure they are packaged and labelled so as not to arouse suspicion and be a target for those who would pilfer lockers for supplies. So in this case, OPSEC and Grey Man would be in full effect. Also, buy quality padlocks for your locker. Don't go to Home Depot – go to a locksmith or online and buy a heavy-duty, high-security lock to secure your locker with.

When storing supplies in your apartment, think outside the usual shelf & cabinet paradigm. Look to the hollows of your furniture, under your bed, behind books on the book shelf, inside the cavities of furniture – anywhere where space is unoccupied and available.

With all of the preceding in mind when preparing your apartment or condo-type living space for an event, you can get it done and can make it effective. All you need to do is put forth the time and effort to do it.

Don; t get caught in a bad situation just because you live in a small box in the sky. You can fortify your living situation and make it far more robust. Build that resilience. Be ready.

SPECIAL CONSIDERATIONS

Invariably, your situation will be unique. There are no two identical preparation scenarios. Everyone lives in a different place, has differing family and group situations, abilities, financial means, skills and experiences. You will have to think clearly and critically how to best prepare for whatever you are preparing for.

Keep in mind the ages and abilities of your group. Very old? Very young? Allergies? Injuries or disabilities? Pets? Medical status (sick, diabetic, pregnant, infirm)? Who has what skills? Medical/food & cooking, mechanical & electrical repairs? Structural carpentry skills? Improvisation? Taking stock of who knows what and how to best utilize it should be done well in advance or, at the very least, as soon as possible from the onset of the situation.

Try to build a small supply of essential emergency supplies to give you a leg up on everyone around you. Have a few cans of fuel around that would give each of your vehicles a full tank. Have a stash of cash hidden somewhere in your home to be ready in the event of a power failure where debit systems, ATMs and banks are no longer able to dispense cash. In desperate times, cash is always king. Keep as much as you feel comfortable or are able. Also, consider a small amount of cash for each vehicle glove box – in case you run out of fuel or need cash in an emergency (just don't keep it with your ownership – you might forget and give the police officer the wrong idea).

Practice your plan in advance. This ensures that everyone knows what needs to be done in case something happens. Everyone in your plan should know how to use everything and should also be aware of everyone else's responsibilities.

Employ a Buddy System – know where your family, friends or team members are and keep tabs on one another in case someone get in trouble and needs help.

Example: An emergency event happens and you and your spouse are at work on opposite ends of the city. The kids are in school. Who goes where and does what? Do the kids know who is supposed to pick them up? Can you contact them via cell or text? Do you have emergency rendezvous points that the kids know how to get to if the bus/subway isn't working? What about extended family and friends? Does everyone know their roles?

HAVE A PLAN. KNOW THE PLAN. WORK THE PLAN.

Remember to have a supply of "luxury items", or what one of my friends calls "snivel gear". Think toilet paper (though you'd be surprised how important it becomes when you can't go buy more. Having a stock of it in the house that gets topped-up rather than refilled is a more efficient practice to get into, that way you will always have a supply at home if the lights go out). A deck of cards, toys for the kids, board games, books to read, maybe a crank radio to power an MP3 player to hear some music to lift spirits. Things like Kool -aid powder as a treat, or hard candy. Ear plugs to help you sleep at night. Eye drops, chap stick, More toilet paper. After 3 days of roughing it, kids (an adults too) tend to get cranky and whine about how terrible life has become.

Consider building a network of friends who are of like-mindset and agree to mutual aid and assistance in times of need. Establish plans of what to do in the event of a disaster, what the *"triggers"* will be to activate your plan, and who will do what. Do you leave when a Storm Warning is issued, or do you simply start charging your devices and head out to the store for supplies before everybody else does? If the weather forecast calls for a storm in 3 days, make sure you top off the tank of your car before it hits, while you're out getting supplies to top things off.

Case Study: Ottawa River Valley Floods, Spring 2019

In the Spring of 2019, I was deployed to the Ottawa River valley in Eastern Ontario to support OP LENTUS with the Canadian Armed Forces. We were deployed as a result of extreme flooding in the area which threatened the homes of thousands of residents. As this operation was directly related to flooding, this is the context with which we will examine lessons-learned I hope you can learn from.

The rising water levels along the river were a result of a combination of factors. These included spring melt, record-breaking rains and the release of water periodically from a dam further upstream. This combination, mixed with occasional warm days increasing the melt speed, made for 100-year record water levels.

By the time the river surged to threatening levels, many residents were behind the curve to take action to protect their homes or to evacuate. By the time the Military was called out and responded, many homes were already overcome by rising water levels.

On the ground, my group was staged at CFB Petawawa and I was then sent out to the Town of Westmeath, operating out of the fire hall and community centre there. During our operations, I made several observations, both about things that worked, and things that didn't.

First off, it's not something new that with Spring comes rising water levels. If you live in a flood-prone area, making advanced preparations and being abreast of changing water levels and weather can go a long way in giving you time to deal with impending disaster, namely building sandbag walls and procuring water pumps. Not to mention evacuating and staging food and supplies at an alternate location should you have to leave. Some residents found that, although their homes were relatively safe from rising flood waters, the roads to get to and from their houses became submerged and impassable by regular vehicles, effectively cutting them off from the means to procure supplies and be reached by emergency responders should they need it. One such cluster of residents were cut off. We ended up delivering groceries and drinking water to them on several occasions while conducting welfare checks.

Rising flood waters hit a 100-year high levels, overwhelming residents and destroying homes.

A significant problem faced by responders was the contamination of flood waters with biomaterials from nearby farms and washed-out septic beds. Even wearing gaiters, troops needed to decontaminate following a day out contacting flood waters. This also impacted the residents as many people in the area relied on wells for their drinking water. These same wells immediately became unreliable for clean water once the river rushed in. This then became a problem for them if they chose to stay.

Depending on the area, utilities were being cut off with an aim to safety. Gas and power lines were being shut down by the local utility companies effectively bringing residents to a "dark age" scenario. Due to the flooding, as well as the physical geography, communications were also severely impacted. Cellular service was almost non-existent in the area, and the only internet connections available were at the Command Post and even then, limited to a small corner of the complex, and ultimately unreliable with so many people trying to use it at once. This posed compounding problems with Command & Control, logistics and response. And that was on the Military side. For the residents, they too faced these challenges as well as rising water levels, food shortages and isolation. Those that had either evacuated early or had prepared before the waters broke over the banks were in a far better position than those who had relied on hoping nothing would happen. It became too little, too late once the water rose in the night and people's homes began to flood. Sandbag walls were not adequate at that point to keep the waters away. It was heartbreaking to see the damage and despair while people desperately tried to stop the rising waters. This was matched by the overwhelming sense of community I witnessed by the residents coming together to help one another in ways I'd not even thought of. Some people used boats to get in and out of town to acquire groceries and transport it back to stranded residents. Many of the people in the surrounding area donated food and their energies to feeding the troops while we were there. It was incredible touching to return after a long da to a hot, home-made meal. Most troops would be cold and wet from the contaminated flood waters and the hot plate of food graciously provided boosted morale while providing much-needed calories.

As an example of a preparation plan for people who may find themselves in such a predicament in the future, I would offer the following as a guideline:

- If possible, PRIOR to buying a property, analyze the geography and determine the likelihood of flooding. As the previous owners and neighbors if there have ever, EVER, been floods there. If so, consider your options and also look into flood insurance riders on your property insurance if available to you.

- If your property is not likely to flood but may be cut-off due to flooding, look for alternative routes in and out and pre-position equipment and supplies to support this. In the event of a medical emergency, not having the means to get help can be fatal.

- If your plan is to evacuate or "bug out" in the event of a flood warning, ensure you are able to lock your property down and secure your things in water-resistant containers in a systematic way. Large, heavy-duty plastic totes can be effective in protecting your wares from rising water. Also, know how to turn off utilities and appliances as you leave so as not to endanger your property more as well as utility workers and responders coming after to try and work in the area.

- If you plan on "bugging in", you will need to prepare to be self-sufficient if your utilities become compromised (water supply, electricity, waste/sanitation, gas, food). Depending on the type of property you have, building in redundancies such as solar arrays for power and gas or propane-powered back-up generators should be considered. A back-up stand-alone water purification method (such as a Big Berkeley filter) should be stored should the water source/well be compromised. Captured water from a water barrel can be used, and, if desperate, boiling combined with a filter may allow for captured water to be made potable.
- Vigilance and awareness of your local geography coupled with a pro-active mindset regarding relevant threats can give you a chance to set-up your defenses or make good your evacuation.
- Ensure you are in-the-know about local news and weather as well as a back-up for communications, consider both a weather radio and a handheld CB/VHF. Learn how to use them and keep extra batteries or ways to charge them.
- Keep a supply of non-perishable foods along with a few cases of drinking water should you need to access it. Rotate them through and keep it fresh. Store what you eat so it's not a hardship to switch gears.
- If you take medications, keep extras on-hand should you become stuck and can't get out or help can't get in.
- If you are in a flood-prone area, pre-position sandbags and associated tools on your property to ensure ready access for a

quick response. And if not for you, consider doing it for your neighbours and how you might help them.
- Be aware, make a plan, work that plan, and be ready.

I thank the residents of Westmeath, Ontario for their hospitality and generosity during my time in their township. You made all the difference, I'm just sorry we couldn't do more.

The Author (right) during Operation LENTUS 2019 – Ottawa River Valley, Ontario, Canada.

Evacuation: When Staying Put is No Longer an Option

There may come a point where remaining in your home is not the wisest choice and you will be forced to decide whether to hunker down and ride it through(bug-in) or evacuate the area, taking your preparedness supplies with you (bug-out). Either you have forewarning of an impending disaster (like a hurricane, flood or massive winter storm) or you hunkered down in the initial stages of an event and the situation has become untenable and leaving is safer (like in the aftermath of an earthquake. It may not be a happy choice to make, but, if you consider the circumstances and your options, it may be the best choice.

The most ideal situation in this is to have a safe place to go to that is ready to receive you (and your party if needed) that is:

- Outside of the disaster area and not affected by it;
- Is capable of sheltering, feeding, supplying and securing you;
- Is secure in itself and not known to others who may try to go there as well and take advantage of it;
- Occupied by "friendly forces", like family or close friends, that you can trust and are like-minded with their own preparations in place;
- Prepared to defend itself from unwelcome hostile visitors.

If you have this, you're laughing. Unfortunately, most people won't have access to an option like this. Bugging out on your own without a defined destination is a gamble.

For one, you will ned to transition from your static location (your already prepped and fortified home) to a mobile platform (likely your car/van/truck) with all your essentials and yourself. You'll then have to contend with everything that goes into traversing and making your way out of an urban centre. If you drive a small car, you have to pre-plan what you'll be taking with you from your apartment, and what you'll leave behind. You'll also have to take additional measures to ensure your vehicle is always ready to go, maintained, fueled up (with extra fuel pre-positioned in case the gas stations go down) and have paper maps (because they don't run on electricity) with pre-marked routes to get to where you're going (which you should have pre-chosen and reconnoitered. For example, one of my plans includes a town outside of my city where I would meet at a specific place in that town at a specific time if I were to signal an evacuation. My family (extended family included) knows the plan and it's particulars, and we know what we are all bringing to the table in that rendezvous. From there, we will have all of our needs met, at least for a month or so.

Look to do the same. Think ahead as to what can happen and plan for that. If it doesn't, at least you had the insurance in place.

"It's better to be a warrior in a garden, than a gardener in a war".

-Unknown

ADDITIONAL CONSIDERATIONS & FOOD FOR FUTURE THOUGHT

➤ Consider becoming competent in some form of self-defense. Your preparedness supplies and infrastructure will be highly coveted post-event, to the extent that after a few days without food some may become desperate enough to kill you for them. Without societal norms and the Rule of Law being enforced some people revert to their savage selves and will take advantage of others when times get tough. This includes everything from un-armed training, to owning various weapons and firearms and being trained on their effective use. This is a personal choice and must be researched on your own. Consider your jurisdictions laws regarding self-defense and weapons use.

➤ Speaking of laws, if you plan to own or possess (and carry) any tools or devices relating to lock entry or bypass (such as lock picks, bypass tools, locksmith equipment and the like) ensure that you review the laws of your jurisdiction or the one you'll be possessing the tools in so as to be aware of what your legal exposure or responsibilities may be. Consult competent independent legal advice on this. True North Tradecraft Ltd, nor the Author make any claims as to the legalities of proposed actions or advice and such information is to be taken as opinion and not legal fact.

➢ If you are a dependent on anything – coffee, cigarettes, etc., you may want to ensure a supply and means to have it. For coffee, an extra pound or two of beans (or ground) a manual bean grinder, stove-top brewing option (like a Bialetti moka espresso pot) and sugar/whitener and a proper little espresso cup. There are other options, like a French Press, and even others like a Handpresso pressure-powered espresso maker (all you need is hot water). If you're a smoker, you might want to store away a few cartons just in case, but you may look into something like nicotine patches or gum because cigarette smoke scent carries and, if you're smoking, that means you have them. This may draw unwanted attention your way and paint you as a target for others looking to take your resources. In a densely packed community like a condo or apartment, the fewer people who know your business (respecting your level of preparedness) the better. Practice you OPSEC and enjoy your coffee.

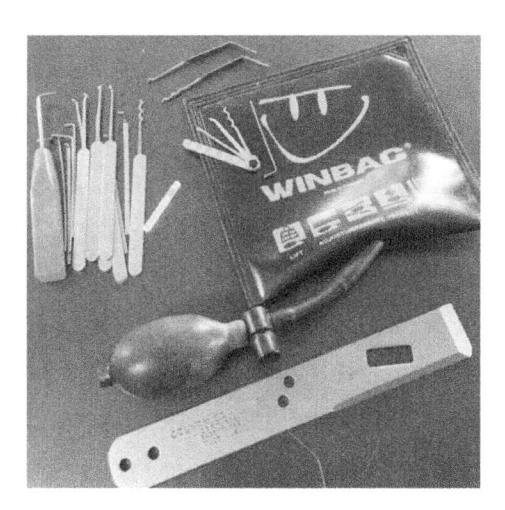

An example of entry tools (left) which can facilitate non-destructive entry in an emergency.

PANDEMIC MEASURES SUPPLEMENT

The events of the past while have caused a great deal of unease as well as panic on a global scale. The COVID-19 Novel Coronavirus has quickly circled the globe and few nations have been unaffected as of this writing.

A pandemic is defined as:

*The **CDC** defines a **pandemic** as "an epidemic that has spread over several countries or continents, usually affecting a large number of people." ... Phase 5: human-to-human transmission in at least two countries within a single WHO region.*

When it comes to preparations for an event such as a Pandemic, many pf the same principles apply.

We need to ensure that our health, welfare and security are established and maintained.

In the beginning phases of a pandemic response, governments at all levels, as well as international Non-Governmental Organizations (NGOs) will be monitoring developments, infection & mortality rates, as well as migration patterns and recovery statistics in an effort to learn more about the disease. IN this process, we have seen that, with a fast-moving virus such as COVID-19, international travel has been affected drastically, to the point of border closures.

As some jurisdictions impose curfews, others are opting to enhance communications with its citizens with best practices to reduce the rate of infection among its population centres.

Here in Canada, the following protocols and best-practices have been put out by the Public Health Agency of Canada so that members of the public can still carry on without massive impacts to their health and safety. In the case of Pandemic preparedness, prevention and preparedness is far more effective initially to curb the spread than dealing with treatment. Some best practices for prevention are:

- Practice Social Distancing: this is the practice of isolating one's self from other people. Staying home, away from gatherings of larger groups of people, essentially spending as much time away from others as possible. Venturing out only for essentials, such as groceries, medicine and essentials. Social distancing should be maintained at a distance of at least 2 metres (or 6 feet) between yourself and anyone who is coughing or sneezing. This is because when someone coughs or sneezes, they spray small liquid droplets from their nose or mouth which may contain the virus. If you are too close, you stand a chance that you can breathe in the droplets, including the COVID-19 virus, if the person coughing has the disease.
- Wash Your Hands: This may seem like common sense, but really, it's not that common. Most viruses and disease is transmitted through the touching of contaminated surfaces or objects, and then touching one's face, mouth, nose, eating food, etc., and then contracting the disease that way. Usually it's just bacteria (like E. Coli, eewww) which can survive on non-biological surfaces longer than viruses, but in the case of COVID-19, the virus can survive on an outside surface for up to 5 days. This means that if you grab a door knob, then rub your

nose or eat a pastry with that dirty hand 5 days after someone carrying the disease touched that same door knob, you may become infected. Use alcohol-based hand sanitizer as a good cleanser, but also remember that regular liquid and bar soap and warm water, scrubbed vigorously for 20-60 seconds, will do the trick without stripping away the natural oils in your hands which help to prevent viral absorption. So, wash your hands. A lot.

- Muffle Your Cough: If you have to cough or sneeze, don't just let fly, use the crook of your arm or a tissue to capture that sneeze. If you used a tissue, discard it right away to avoid contaminating things further.
- Sanitize Your Area: Your home should be sterilized. Door handles, hard surfaces, dishes, YOUR PHONE, remote controls, anything that you touch on the regular where you don't wash your hands BEFORE you touch it.
- Avoid Touching your Eyes, Nose and Mouth: This is important because, once contaminated, your hands can transfer the virus to your eyes, nose and mouth. From there, the virus can enter your body and can make you sick. Assume that you have virus on your hands – like wet paint – and everywhere you go you leave paint behind. Dirty, virus-y paint. If you can imagine that, then ensure that no paint is left behind. Clean, sanitize and ensure that you wash your hands regularly before, during and after cleaning up. That way you can control cross-contamination and reduce the chances of getting sick.
- If Needed, Seek Medical Care Early: Stay home if you feel unwell. If you develop a fever, cough and difficulty breathing, seek medical attention and call ahead that you will be coming. That way, the hospital or clinic will be prepared to receive you and process you quickly while observing procedures to minimize further contamination while getting you treatment

ahead of those triaged at lower risk. Also, calling ahead may enable an overcrowded hospital from directing you to a less busy facility which would ease the burden on wait times as resources dwindle.

- Practice Food Safety: As you should already, ensure that your foods are properly handled, washed and cooked to ensure you not only don't get COVID-19, but also other sicknesses which can weaken your immune system, reducing your immune system against Coronavirus.
- Stock appropriate medicines (Tylenol, Advil, children's medicines, cough suppressants, anti-diarrhea and anti-nauseants, first aid supplies and multi-vitamin & mineral supplements.

To keep things clean, items like bleach, Clorox (wipes & spray), alcohol (over %70), liquid and regular bar soap go a long way.

For the most part, health authorities are no longer endorsing the use of masks for healthy individuals, though some requirements are still in place for certain settings in Canada. Much of this reason is that the masks themselves may not be used and fitted properly, thereby creating a false sense of security for the wearer. Also, if the mask becomes contaminated, just by taking it off you may contaminate your hands, leading to infection through touch.

If you do choose to wear a mask as you venture nearer to other people (at a grocery store or pharmacy), then you may look at wearing gloves while out and discarding them safely as you re-enter your home, as well as washing and sanitizing your mask inside and out with an alcohol-based sanitizer or soap and hot water. Remember that removable filters reach a saturation point at which they are no longer effective at filtering.

As a recommendation for a mask, I would look at 3M and their respirators or another reputable company like MIRA Safety. Anything that isn't actually fitted and sealed to your face is not actually filtering the air but presenting a barrier for you to suck in air around. I was given the following recommendations from a technician at 3M regarding virus and bacterial contaminants as to which mask and filter combos are appropriate:

Respirator

Full – FF-400 series respirator (~$250)

Or

Half – 750-#(size 1, 2 or 3) (~$35)

Filter

3M 2091 (P100) particulate filter (~$6/pr)

or

3M 60926 cartridge (combo) (~$12/pr)

When it comes to stocking up, racing out to buy 8 million rolls of toilet paper and a truck load of beef jerky does nothing for you. Think of what you would normally use for 3-6 weeks. But don't get all of it. Your government's primary focus, after slowing the spread of the virus and keep hospitals running, is to ensure the integrity of the supply chain for food, medicine and other essentials like fuel and parts for utilities and services.

As long as critical infrastructure remains operational – the taps keep running, the lights stay on and trucks keep rolling – most of the issues surrounding your ability to stay fed, warm, clean and free from infection are covered. If you don't have to venture out, don't.

One thing learned from the pandemic has been the importance of community and teamwork. Working together, in small, mutually-supportive groups of people who keep to themselves and help one another can minimize the risks of catching a sickness while lightening the burden of isolation. Different people bring different strengths to a group and make up for areas or gaps in the ability to prosper. Stockpiling may be too expensive for one person or family, but several people sharing their stockpiled resources (trading essentials to one another) allows for diversification of resources. For instance: someone who has a lot of flour and can bake, and another who has veggies and can garden can share with one another so they both have bread and veggies. If someone is good with preserving meats and others are good with providing the materials to do so (both preserving materials and the meat itself), both can prosper from the arrangement as the time and effort and knowledge required to preserve is a commodity like money is. Trade of this sort can lighten the burden of going it alone. Use your skills and help one another in the ways of health, wellness, food, security and charity, without sacrificing your own safety or survival.

Preparedness Recommendations

- Bare-bones Emergency Kit (tailor according to # of people)
- Extra clothing, blankets and/or sleeping bag per person.
- Hats & gloves, rain gear, sturdy shoes or boots,
- Flashlights & batteries (per person), some candles & a lighter; stove to cook food camp stove & fuel.
- Bottled water, water purification tablets or liquid.
- Non-perishable easy-to-prepare food adequate for your group (w/ manual can opener, pot to boil water & food).
- First aid training course, first aid kit & reserve medications if needed.
- Self-contained, portable, solar or hand-powered radio.
- Antiseptic baby wipes, hand sanitizer and rubbing alcohol
- Plastic tarps or sheeting.
- Sturdy full-tang knife, multi-tool, duct-tape, small sharpener, WD-40, small tool kit.
- Length of rope/cord/paracord (25-50 feet).
- Photocopies of all important documents (Will, insurance, passports & IDs, important contact info, computer backups – Hardcopy, scanned to cloud and on a USB key).
- Bottle of bleach, hand sanitizer, heavy-duty garbage bags, all in a plastic pail.

- All items to be kept in a well-marked, dedicated container or bag in an easily accessible place.
- Tools to affect repairs and turn off/on utilities.
- Some entertainment items to maintain morale.
- Accessible security items.
- Ability to secure your home (plywood for windows, 2×4s, hammer, nails).
- Back-up power source with solar panels if possible.
- Copy of your family emergency plan, map, compass.
- Emergency cash, in small and medium bills.
- Coffee. (I prefer Arrowhead Coffee's Cleared Hot espresso)

Websites Of Note:

- **True North Tradecraft Ltd.** – Training, Blog and online store addressing personal security tradecraft and resilience topics, training and specialized gear. Providing personal security training to civilians and counter-custody & covert entry training to Military and Law Enforcement. Contact us to book / host a workshop, read our informative posts, buy quality gear and join our community in our quest to build resilience and self-reliance amongst as many people as we can. Veteran-owned & operated in Toronto, Canada.

www.truenorthtradecraft.ca (Follow us on Facebook, Instagram, Google+, YouTube and LinkedIn as @truenorthtradecraft / Twitter @Ttradecraft)

- **The CORE Group** – a top-tier physical security and covert entry training and consulting firm, based on the US East coast. www.enterthecore.net

- **4TAC5** – providing specialist counter-custody and restraint escape training and specialized equipment to military & law enforcement units. www.4tac5.com and www.oscardelta.com (True North Tradecraft is the authorized stockist and certified trainer for these offerings in Canada.
- **WSC Survival School Inc**. - Providing practical and effective wilderness survival training to all venturing into the out-of-doors. Owned and operated by David Arama, the original instructor of Les "Survivorman" Stroud. http://www.wscsurvivalschool.com/
- **HealthLink BC** – Canadian Provincial medical information service. From their website: "HealthLink BC provides reliable non-emergency health information and advice in British Columbia and available to all. Through their programs and services, you can get the information you need to make decisions for yourself and those you care for. With our website, and telephone service, information is available whenever you want it, anytime day or night, every day of the year". See https://www.healthlinkbc.ca for more.
- **Ed's Manifesto** – Ed is a non-permissive environment & counter-custody specialist and published author with over 12 years of operational experience along the Mexican-American border. His unique approach to training, by incorporating insights of criminal mindset and culture, improvised weapons, austere environment awareness and counter-custody methodologies, creates an immersive learning experience for his students which is not easily forgotten. Find him at www.edsmanifesto.com
- **On-Point Tactical**. Owner/Operator Kevin Reeve has trained everyone from civilians to Tier-1 Special Forces units in

wilderness survival, Emergency Preparedness and tactical operations. Available all across America, see their site www.onpointtactical.com for course calendar and details.
- **Tactikey** – Kick-ass personal security keychain that works. www.tactikey.com.
- **Canadian Tactical Officer's Association** – Canadian-based training consortium for vetted law enforcement, military and select security. http://ctoa.ca/
- **International Tactical Training Association** - Chicago, Illinois-based training provider for law enforcement, government agency and military clients. http://ittaonline.org
- **CTOMS Inc.** - Cutting edge Canadian-based medical training and equipment provider. http://ctoms.ca
- **Delta2Alpha Design** – Providing innovative solutions for fitness and combatives training as well as equipment. Canadian provider at https://delta2alpha.com/.
- **Vinjatek** – Former covert operative & nomad John V. Cain shares loads of information about tradecraft, travel, security and gear. The subscription is well worth it - see https://vinjatek.com.
- **Government of Canada** – Get Prepared website: includes tips and resources to better understand preparedness from a Canadian Governmental perspective. https://www.getprepared.gc.ca/
- **United States Federal Emergency Management Agency (FEMA)** – Great resource for various disaster and preparedness considerations along with government policies and related documents. https://www.fema.gov
- **Recoil: OFFGRID Magazine** – 6 issues per year covering the latest in preparation & survival topics. Note, this is an American

publication and all of its topics may not be applicable to a contemporary Canadian context. That said, the information is top-notch and is relevant and applicable worldwide. Subscriptions available to Canada and internationally at www.offgridweb.com .

- **PrepareCenter.Org** – Red Cross/Crescent-based website discussing preparedness with a worldwide scope, referencing a wide spectrum of disasters, issues and geographic areas. Several language profiles are supported, as well as hundreds of other resources. There are even Apps. All free! A fantastic resource. Go to https://www.preparecenter.org/topics/disaster-preparedness for more.
- **Centers for Disease Control and Prevention (CDC)** – A US-based public health agency. A trove of free information, along with an entire section on Emergency Preparedness, Pandemic preparedness and public health issues. https://www.cdc.gov

Further Reading:

- Handbook to Practical Disaster Preparedness for the Family (2nd Edition); Arthur T. Bradley, 2011
- Emergency Food Storage & Survival Handbook; Peggy Layton, 2002
- Preparedness Now; Aton Edwards, 2009
- www.disaster-survival-guide.com; (Emergency kits & multi-tiered strategy)
- Urban & Off the Grid Survival Skills and Preparedness (2nd Edition); David Arama & WSC Survival School, 2013
- When All Hell Breaks Loose; Cody Lundin, 2007, Gibbs Smith Press
- Urban Survival Guide; David Morris, 2009
- When Trucks Stop, America Stops; American Trucking Associations, 2006
- National Outdoor Leadership School's (NOLS) Wilderness Guide; Mark Harvey, Fireside Publishing, 1999.
- Emergency – This Book Will Save Your Life; Neil Strauss, 2009, HarperCollins Publishers.
- Tom Brown's Field Guide – City and Suburban Survival; Tom Brown Jr. with Brant Morgan, Berkley Publishing Group, 1984.
- Prepare For Anything Survival Manual; Tim Macwelch and the Editors of Outdoor Life, Weldon Owen Publishing, 2014.